12/97

D0342499

Time Off From Work

Other Books by Lisa Angowski Rogak

The 100 Best Retirement Businesses

New England Farm Vacations

The Cat on My Shoulder

Vermont: Off the Beaten Path

The Quotable Cat

Latin for Pigs (with Virginia R. Blackert)

The Upstart Guide to Owning and Managing a
Bed & Breakfast

The Upstart Guide to Owning and Managing an
Antiques Business

Time Off From Work

Using Sabbaticals to Enhance Your Life While Keeping Your Career on Track

LISA ANGOWSKI ROGAK

JOHN WILEY & SONS, INC.

New York • Chichester • Brisbane • Toronto • Singapore

Library of Congress Cataloging-in-Publication Data:

Rogak, Lisa Angowski
   Time off from work : using sabbaticals to enhance your life while
keeping your career on track / Lisa Angowski Rogak.
       p. cm.
   Includes index.
   ISBN 0-471-31067-0 (pbk. : acid-free paper)
   1. Leave of absence. 2. Sabbatical leave. I. Title.
HD5255.R64 1995
331.25'763—dc20   94-18143

Printed in the United States.

10 9 8 7 6 5 4 3 2 1

For Dan,
My sabbatical partner in life

Contents

Contents

Contents

Time Off From Work

Introduction

"So, what do you do all day, anyway?"

The questioner was a new acquaintance whom I had met at a booksigning. When I told him I had written several other books and had several more due in the next year, he became curious about what writers actually do with their days.

"You must write twelve hours a day, right?"

I took a deep breath and set out to burst his bubble.

"Well, no," I responded. "I get up when I want—usually around eight or nine, make a pot of coffee, read for an hour or two, and maybe answer a few phone calls. Then I'll do some work outside and go for a run. The mail will have come by that point, so I'll read that. If anything needs my immediate attention, I'll make a few phone calls or write a letter. Then I'll make dinner and spend the evening reading and figuring out what I'm going to do the next day."

He just stared at me.

"Oh, and sometimes I'll head for the library at Dartmouth and do some research or read. Then, as long as I'm out, I'll head for the bookstore to see what's new."

Still nothing.

"But I also might do a couple of phone interviews if I'm working on a book or magazine article, and when I get a new idea for a book, then I'll spend the afternoon writing a proposal." I paused. "When I'm working on a travel book, I spend a lot of time on the road all over New England."

His vital signs had gone south.

"But when I'm under a deadline, that's when I really work."

Finally, signs of life returning.

"Oh yeah? How many hours a day do you work then?"

"Oh, five, six tops."

He threw his signed copy of my book down in disgust. "Lady, you're living like one of those goddamn college perfessers who's always going on sabbatical every other year."

As he stalked off, I thought, "Yeah, I guess I am."

As a writer, I've almost always worked for myself, so I guess it does seem like I live my life as if I'm on permanent sabbatical. I admit I'm incredibly spoiled by my work. It's not always as rosy as I've just made it out to be; but I honestly don't know how the majority of people can work the way they do.

I've always been a big proponent of people taking time off from their regular jobs, even if only for an afternoon. When I lived in New York, I remember calling my friends at their high-rise office complexes and cajoling them into playing hooky with me. To this day, I consider it my civic duty to convince anyone who will listen why they should take a break from work.

Many of you reading this will take time off and then return to your jobs. Perhaps I've gone a little overboard in some sections of this book, assuming that once you manage to extricate yourself from the office for even a short period of time, you'll start to hatch a plot where you can finally be on your own, living without a boss or time clock.

You Already Know How to Take Time Off

Chances are that you already know how to take a sabbatical. Although most people think of a college professor's year off when they hear the term *sabbatical*, I use the word to refer to any type of break from how you normally spend your time, whether it lasts for a month, for several years, or forever.

As Noel Aderer, one of the women interviewed for this book, puts it, "My life is one big sabbatical." Even though my varieties of time off have come in different flavors throughout the years, it is always that all-purpose sabbatical that drives my choice of career and where I choose to live.

My all-purpose sabbatical is my writing—I don't consider any part of my work to be work—and any time I'm writing, I'm learning about something I didn't know about before. They're all subjects that I'm passionately interested in.

Among my friends, I'm famous for my moving sabbaticals. I've lived at more than twenty different addresses in just over twelve years. After spending most of my childhood in the same house, I wanted to be footloose, and I was. My shortest tenure at any address was six weeks; my longest, two years. This sabbatical recently ended when I returned to the town where I finally feel I've grown some roots.

Then there was the sabbatical that I'm sure you're probably more than a little familiar with: the relationship sabbatical. You know, when you swear off men/women/whatever for a certain period of time. Finally there was my moving-to-the-country sabbatical.

My most regular sabbaticals have been my burnout sabbaticals, which usually come after a period of about six solid months of pitching ideas to publications and writing books and pieces for magazines. After the last assignment is handed in and there are no more on the horizon, I just stop what I'm doing and take off. Traveling has always been my favorite way to spend time off, although sometimes it looks like work since I occasionally manage to get a book or two out of it.

Since I've written *Time Off From Work*, I've been amazed at the number of people I've met who've gotten off the merry-go-round for a while, whether they have money or not.

And whenever I casually mention to people that I've written a book on how to take a break from work, I seem to turn into an instant lightning rod for all their dreams and what they are going to do when they a) win the lottery, b) finally tell the boss where to go, and c) start to live the kind of life that they deserve.

Although this kind of fantasy wields an enormous amount of power over the majority of the American population, the truth is that carefully planning your time off—whether it's a sabbatical or family leave—will make you feel like you have much more control over your life. Plus, you don't have to wait for your lucky numbers to hit.

At this point, you're probably thinking it's important to take time off, but then doubts creep in: your boss won't stand for it, you can't afford it, what makes you think you can do this, etc. Believe me, everyone that I interviewed for this book said that this litany of excuses regularly ran through their minds as they planned their sabbaticals, and for some, it even continued through the early part of their time off.

Why? Probably because they sensed that their lives would change drastically as a result of their sabbatical. And the truth is that you certainly will not be the same person you were before your time off. I know I'm not. After I hooked into the pattern of taking periodic breaks from work, I discovered that if I could manage to take a breather every so often, I was probably capable of doing anything I wanted. I've tried a lot of different things over the years, failing, of course, at some projects while succeeding at others.

Exactly how *you'll* change is impossible to predict. Only know that it will happen.

For me, I've found that the time out that I've taken from writing has served to balance my interests and calm me down somewhat. Even though I do consider myself to be on permanent sabbatical, I still have been able to recognize the benefits from the real breaks that I've taken from my work. Sometimes, when you free up your mind from the usual working stresses and think about something else, that's usually when the best ideas crop up. The clamor and chaos of your job was probably enough to drown them out.

And that new idea might be enough to start a new project at work that will earn you a promotion, or else start you on an entirely new career path.

When I slow down, stop combing newspapers and magazines for ideas, and start reading for leisure, I find that the best ideas slam into my brain from out of left field.

For instance, one day, during one of my extended breaks, I was taking a long walk down a remote dirt road lined on both sides by sizable dairy farms. It was a gorgeous spring day, and the road was still muddy in parts, but I felt so lucky at that moment that I thought, "Why can't everyone be doing this right now?"

Thus was born the idea for *Time Off From Work*, and you're holding it in your hands right now.

1

Why Take Time Off?

Martha Owens of Manchester, Tennessee, was burned out. After working as a legal administrator for 24 years, 10 hours a day or more, she needed a break. "I really love what I do," she said, "but the 50- and 60-hour weeks were making me hate it."

Owens thought that taking two months off one summer to go to southwestern Colorado would give her the time away from the office that she needed. "Basically, I needed to learn how to relax, because with my job, I didn't know how," she said. She contacted a couple of friends who ran a summer ranch resort in Colorado and arranged with them to trade some chores for a cabin of her own and meals for July and August.

When she first approached her boss about taking the time off, he flatly refused. "I went back to him six weeks later, and again and again, and kept on him until he agreed that I could take the leave without pay," she says.

Owens said that her boss initially turned down her request because he was afraid that she wouldn't come back. "I told him that I had to come back because I have to make a living. He let me go because he knew that I was going to go anyway, even if it meant that I would quit my job. So I went." She added, "But it was not with his blessing."

She started planning for her sabbatical even before she asked her boss for the time off. Owens paid her rent and some of her bills in advance and began to save money for traveling expenses. "It took a lot of discipline to do everything at the same time. I was really cutting corners," she says. But the advantage was that she wouldn't need to spend any money while she was away: her room and board were covered and the owners of the ranch also would give her $200 in compensation at the end of the summer.

Owens helped train a woman to fill in for her at the law office for five of the weeks she would be gone. However, she could see problems with the arrangement even before she left. "It was hard for me to let go of the quality of work, because I knew it wasn't going to be done the way I would have done it," she said.

Her coworkers and friends encouraged her to go, as did her children, but her parents thought she was crazy. "My mother thought that I wouldn't come back," she said.

Her hesitations aside, Owens left for her trip in July of 1992. Her destination was the Thirty Mile Ranch in Creede, Colorado. She spent her two months cooking and cleaning a few hours a day and talking with the guests. The rest of the time she walked through the mountains, relaxed, and set aside time for reading and Bible study. "At home, I found that my mind was so clogged up that I could never do things like that," she said. "It made me realize that you have to set aside certain times at home for yourself and let nothing else get in the way."

The summer flew by, and Owens says that the only reason she came back to Tennessee was that she missed her two grandchildren, who live in the same town. If it weren't for them, however, she would have probably found a place out west to work. She did stop in at a law firm in Santa Fe and made some contacts in Colorado Springs, but in the end, she said, she couldn't have moved out there because she's not fond of the cold weather.

Once she returned to her job, Owens was unprepared for the amount of work that had piled up in her absence, but she was able to convince her boss to hire a secretary to help her dig herself out. Even so, it wasn't until November that her routine at the office returned to normal, but she was determined to work without putting in a lot of overtime as she had in the past.

While she was out in Colorado, Owens frequently thought about what she could do to help keep her motivated once she returned to her job. She decided that taking two months off every year fit the bill.

"My boss told me that he can't have a part-time secretary who's going to be away two months every year, but each year he's going to have to go through the same thing," she said. "You know, he never even asked me about my trip to Colorado; in fact, he told me once that he didn't want to hear about it at all. But I'm going to prevail upon him again, and I feel that after I've worked for him for so long, I'm entitled to the time off.

"It took a lot of courage, and it took me being stubborn, making up my mind that I was going to do it no matter what," she said. "For someone who is devoted to her job and a workaholic to boot, time off is the only thing that was going to save me. I just wish I had the guts ten years ago to do this, because I think I would be calmer and more serene now."

Owens adds that even though she worried about what would happen at the office in her absence, she knew that once she left, the situation was out of her control. "The point is that you're still the employee and they're still the employer, and they're going to do what they're going to do whether you're there or not. If it takes two years to plan for it, do it for yourself," she says. "I was raised in the old school, that when you're doing things for yourself, you're being selfish, but it's not true. Taking the time off was the very best thing I've ever done for myself."

Time Off: A Growing Trend

In her book *The Popcorn Report* (Doubleday 1991), trend forecaster Faith Popcorn calls sabbaticals "the luxury vacation of the 90s." In a 1990 poll conducted for the magazine *Special Report*, 64 percent of respondents aged 25 to 49 reported that they regularly dreamed about quitting their jobs to go off and do something else for a while. Their dreams ranged from something as hedonistic as traveling around the world to living on a desert island. Nineteen percent of respondents aged 35 to 49 said they think about taking time off from work at least once a day.

Sabbaticals have been a perennial favorite of academics for years. In fact, some professors have even admitted that one of the primary reasons they chose their profession is that they get to take off one year out of every seven; in essence, it is this prospect that keeps the headaches of the other six years tolerable.

Laypeople, or nonacademics, tend to think of time off for themselves only in terms of the standard issue two-week vacation, month of maternity leave, or enforced "sabbatical" that comes in between jobs.

Time off during the 1980s was almost unthinkable. With an economy that grew by leaps and bounds and a real estate market that followed suit, no one wanted to miss out. The recession of the nineties created the corporate triumvirate of downsizing, early retirement, and reduced working hours. As a result, many people began to question their loyalty to corporations that thought nothing of cutting 2,000 "sticky-floor" jobs at a pop while increasing the salaries and bonuses of those safely ensconced high above the glass ceiling.

Paralleling these trends is the fact that the bulk of the baby boomers are nearing and passing the magic age of 40, causing them to re-examine both their priorities and their frenzied commitment to work. For them, a sabbatical is time off to figure out what's next. Some will want to take time off to recommit themselves to their jobs; others will decide that it's not too late to move to Vermont and raise llamas.

What people are doing with their sabbaticals and family leaves is a huge mixed bag: some go back to school while others write books, start businesses, or travel. Most people take the time off by themselves, but a few have arranged for the whole family to join them.

Why Are People More Interested in Taking Time Off?

Most people, when asked if they would like to take a break from work, respond with, "Sure," a stupid grin, and a mind that starts racing with thoughts of all the things they'd like to do if only they had the time, money, and inclination. However, they usually cut themselves off by thinking of all of the reasons why they can't take time off.

But they think about sabbaticals anyway, even though most of the time it's only a useless fantasy designed to get them through a boring day or help them deal with a demanding or incompetent boss. The fact is that more people are thinking about taking a break from work and here's why:

You see the need for a balanced life. Men and women have recently begun to see that work isn't everything. They want to better integrate their professional working and personal lives, and taking a sabbatical is one big way to get a jump start.

You want to do what you want for a change. Even though several generations of Americans have been unfairly branded as selfish, the truth is that many people—especially women—are more selfless than the media make them out to be. Here, too, is the need for balance: In order to appreciate your giving side, you have to give to yourself as well. Taking time off is a great way to start.

You're tired of hitting the glass ceiling or remaining on the sticky floor. If you haven't already made it to where you think you should be by now, then your chances probably aren't that great of ever reaching the upper echelons of your company or industry—not as long as you work for someone else. As job opportunities in traditional occupations decrease, many people are having to look for employment outside the usual realms. Feeling stuck is one thing that propels some people toward seeking a break; but once they're out there, they see a wide variety of opportunities they weren't aware of in a company where progress is solely linear. These people often end up switching to a company or a career where there is more opportunity.

Admit it. Your health isn't what it used to be. Granted, the baby-boomer generation—which comprises a great majority of the people who are putting their lives under the kind of scrutiny that often leads to a sabbatical—is a hardy bunch. But if you're in that group, you're getting older, which means you're slowing down. Ten or even five years ago, you could easily pull an all-nighter at the office without adverse effects. Now, you may start thinking about switching to a career that is not as stressful. A sabbatical provides a wonderful way to examine a number of options without having to commit to them first.

You want to explore a particular interest. When you're young and idealistic, it's easy to envision yourself in a glamorous career by the age of 25. In most cases, of course, real life intercedes, and the need to make a living pushes your dream to the back burner, where it remains, sometimes until retirement, if it even manages to resurface at that time at all.

But sometimes, everyday life just becomes too much to bear, what with the job, the family, and the bills, and you say to yourself, "Goddamm it, I work hard. Why shouldn't I be able to do what I want?" So you manage a six-month break from work to get back in touch with your "first" career, and you realize that you never really lost your love for it after all. And so you begin your avocation—or vocation—anew.

More women are refusing to buy into the corporate structure that many men secretly hate. As millions of women poured into the mainstream labor markets in the 1970s and 1980s, entering through doors that were originally closed to them, some immediately saw all the warts. A few left, but most stayed. Some even thought the warts were their own.

But for those women who stayed, things didn't get much better. In addition, many male bosses still think that women employees are more dispensable then men, because they figure most women will just get pregnant anyway.

So they find they can't win and decide to leave. This situation, along with the increasing number of women who are unwilling to put up with corporate inequities, means that more women leave jobs than men. Witness the growing number of women who are starting their own businesses in proportions twice as large as those for men.

There is no doubt that at least one of your reasons for wanting to take time off is given in the list above. Some of you might even agree with every item on the list, but you remain convinced that the best thing to do is to suffer in silence because you need your job, the economy's tight, and so on.

Don't be like this. Once you declare your intentions to take time off for yourself, most of the negative reactions that you'll receive will be from people who see your desire for a leave as disturbing the status quo. "What makes you think that you're better than the rest of us?" a spokesperson for the group might say. "Why do you think you have what it takes to just up and leave?"

But you're not just like the rest, as evidenced by your taking steps to live the kind of life that suits *you*, not everybody else. Keep going in your pursuit of taking a sabbatical. Read about how others have dealt with people who wanted to see them fail, and see what a bit of time off from the grind will ultimately mean to your life.

Now figure out which of the following applies to you: You like your job, but need a break; you've been working in your career too long and would like some time off, but you also want to look for another job; or, you want to be more active on your sabbatical and travel for an extended period of time.

If you're considering a sabbatical, you should get excited, because in this book, you'll find not only a variety of case histories—more than 40 people from all career areas—but solid how-to information on everything you need to start planning for your time off. This book will take you through the entire process, from how to focus on what you want to do, to finding the money for it, to telling your boss so long, you're off for three months. The idea is to get to the point where you feel like your life is "one big sabbatical," so start planning it. If you've always dreamed about taking some time off from the grind to do what *you* want to do for a change, here's how to do it.

Four Basic Models

The term *sabbatical* is used here as a broad term for time off, whether it's paid or unpaid, one month or one year. Although some of the people profiled in the book were quick to say that they didn't really take a sabbatical, they also tended to spend their time off working harder than they ever did at any job, or use the traditional academic definition of a sabbatical and take off less than a year. When companies offer a formal program of paid leaves to their employees, they most often refer to the leave as a sabbatical, whereas an unpaid leave is referred to as, well, an unpaid leave.

No matter what they called it, however, everyone in this book took a sabbatical as defined here: a well-deserved break from the ordinary working grind.

There are four different kinds of sabbaticals:

1. *Paid Leave.* This is most frequently offered for a set period of time to employees in top management, or to all employees after they've been with the company for a certain number of years. Benefits such as health insurance and corporate investment contributions to pension funds and IRAs usually continue, and the worker's position is almost always held open until she returns. The most common time frame of paid leaves is from six weeks to four months.

2. *Unpaid Leave.* Many companies have a formal or informal policy stating that an employee can take an unspecified amount of time off for personal reasons, which can range from the need for more time than the average two-week vacation provides, to caring indefinitely for an ailing parent. The latter category would now fall under the Family Medical Leave Act. An unpaid leave can last from a month or two up to several years, and placement in the same job usually is not guaranteed by the company, especially with lengthy leaves.

3. Social Service Leave. This is a leave that's sometimes counted as part of a company's community service program. One example would be an employee who takes time off to work in a shelter for the homeless or some other nonprofit pursuit. When granted under an established social service program, these leaves are almost always fully salaried with all benefits continuing. The employee returns to the same job. When a company doesn't have a formal social service program, an employee must then take this time under the auspices of an unpaid leave.

4. Voluntary Work-Reduction Leave. This is akin to what happens when an airplane is overbooked, and you trade your seat for one on a later flight and a few goodies in return. Sometimes, when a company needs to cut its workforce for a specified period of time, management will ask for volunteers and throw in a few sweeteners like continued benefits, tuition reimbursement, and guaranteed placement when they call you back. Of course, a job is guaranteed—along with all of the sweeteners—if the company is still around, but usually it's the job of the company's choice, not yours.

The Top Five Myths about Sabbaticals

1. You won't come back. Admittedly, there are people who don't return from a leave of absence, but in most cases, a sabbatical builds loyalty among employees: "If the company cares that much about me to give me time off," goes the reasoning, "I'd better appreciate it."

2. Taking time off is the equivalent of a demotion at work. Untrue. Although some people fear "out of sight, out of mind" is the rule when it comes to the workplace, most of your coworkers and managers will be eager to find out how they can take time off too, especially in a company without a formal leave program. For this reason, they're unlikely to alienate you.

3. You'll get lazy. Some of your coworkers might notice that when you return, you're not the workaholic you were before you took time off. That's their view, but what usually happens is that you get a good sense of your priorities while you're away from the office for an extended period of time and prefer to spend your postsabbatical evenings with your family instead of your colleagues. This might mean that the guy who works 60 hours a week to your 45 may get the next VP slot that opens up, but it probably won't really bother you since you've gained a new perspective.

4. It'll set your career back. Many people think that career counselors and potential bosses look upon a break in resumes as bad news. In some cases, that's true, even though you can usually explain that you were looking for a job. But designing your own sabbatical shows initiative that is unusual in workers today, so go ahead and put it on your resume. It'll probably be a plus and get a lot of attention. Hint: Go into detail about the variety of skills you had to call upon to save for and then plan your sabbatical from start to finish. Prospective employers will be impressed. And it's a great conversation piece.

5. You can't afford it. This is the most common excuse given for why someone won't even consider taking time off from work, but it's usually the easiest problem to solve. If you make up your mind that you are going to take a sabbatical, you'll find a way to finance it.

The Top Five Truths about Sabbaticals

1. It will change your life. Anything you do that allows you the chance to both step back from your life and exercise your independence will have enormous ramifications for the rest of your life, even if you return to the same lifestyle after your sabbatical ends.

2. *Your sabbatical will make you both more independent and more dependent.* Whether or not you think you're already pretty independent, having an extended period of time off will make you realize that you're capable of much more than you were previously aware. At the same time, you will probably get a clearer perspective on humanity, because you are either working more closely with people or are getting away from the teeming masses for a while, and it's a good bet that you'll begin to appreciate people again.

3. *It will be challenging.* Even if it sounds simple—"Imagine, having two months off to weave baskets!"—the challenge will develop when you go looking for it under your own motivation and not because someone else is telling you to.

4. *It will be one of the most satisfying things you'll ever do for yourself.* You will accomplish many things in your life, but because a sabbatical is entirely self-directed, the sense of achievement you'll have at the end will be nothing like any work project you've ever completed.

5. *If you plan to take time off and then don't, you'll always wonder.* And if you're the kind of person who is dreaming now, this is even more likely.

Why Do *You* Want to Take Time Off?

Everyone has his or her own reasons for wanting to take a breather from the rat race that is the modern workplace, but before you decide how you want to spend your time off, you should evaluate exactly why you want to leave. If you do it for the wrong reasons—to get away from an abusive boss, for instance—chances are good that you won't get the full benefit from your leave, because something besides your own desire is fueling it.

Even though you may already have a good idea of why you want to take a sabbatical, answering the following questions will help you focus on your true motivations. It's a good idea to get a notebook so you can start planning your sabbatical in detail. Throughout the course of this book, you'll have the opportunity to ask yourself about different aspects of your sabbatical, from how you envision your time off to how you're going to pay for it. Answer as honestly as you can the questions that appear here and in subsequent chapters, going into as much detail as you need. Keep your answers in mind as you read the following chapters.

1. Why do you want to take a sabbatical? Write down five answers and rank them in order of importance.

2. How much time do you think you'll need?

3. What do you want to know at the end of your leave that you don't know now?

4. What do you like about your job?

5. What do you dislike about your job?

6. What do you want to accomplish during your time off from work?

7. What would you like to do if there was nothing to stand in your way?

8. Do you want your sabbatical to be for you alone, or would you like your family to join you?

9. What's your biggest excuse for not taking time off from work?

10. If you knew you had six months off from work and money wasn't an issue, how would you spend your time?

11. If you knew you had six months off from work but money was an issue, how would you spend your time?

BRAINSTORM: Quickly make a list of 25 things you'd like to do. Write them down even if they make no sense. Then cross out your least favorite.

How Does the New Family Medical Leave Act Affect You?

The Family Medical Leave Act that President Clinton signed into law in 1993 has had enormous ramifications for employees who want to take time off from work because of their own or a family member's medical problems. The act, arguably Clinton's first far-reaching piece of legislation, requires that companies with more than 50 employees provide up to 12 weeks of unpaid leave within the course of a year for any employee who requests it *and* can prove the need, usually with a note from a doctor and occasionally a second opinion. Under the act, the reasons for taking a leave include childbirth for the mother and the father, the need to care for a family member with a serious illness, or the employee's own illness. When the employee returns to work, the company must give the worker his or her old job back, or an equivalent position within the company, if the previous job has already been filled. The company must also provide continuing health coverage and other benefits for the employee during the leave. Even though some corporations and industries have predicted that the economic cost of the act for business will be staggering, the Bureau of Labor

Statistics says that out of 50 million male and female workers who are eligible to take advantage of the law, a small percentage—only 2.5 million—will actually pursue a leave each year.

Unless you work for a business with 50 or more permanent, full-time employees, you're not covered by the act. According to the Bureau of Labor Statistics, while 96 percent of American businesses have fewer than 50 workers, only 34 percent of the American workforce works for these companies.

In addition, a business may refuse a leave to an employee who falls in the category of the company's top 10 percent most highly paid workers, if the company can claim that the employee's absence would cause irreparable damage to the economic health of the business.

According to the Long Island, New York, chapter of the employment advocate group 9 to 5, it's rumored that some employers have been undertaking shady policies to avoid the costs of the law, including firing pregnant women staffers before the act took effect, or hiring a surplus of temporary workers in order to keep the permanent payroll below 50. However, most companies that are affected are accepting the consequences of the law.

Top Ten Reasons Why People Want to Take Time Off from Work

1. They're not challenged at work.

2. Their fingerprints are all over the glass ceiling.

3. They need a breather from routine.

4. They want to try living in the country for a while.

5. They hate their bosses.

(Continued)

(Continued)

6. They want to call the shots.

7. They want to switch jobs.

8. They want to travel.

9. They want to start their own businesses.

10. They've decided that working 70 hours a week isn't the way they want to live.

Getting Creative: It Doesn't Have to Look a Certain Way

An employee who really wants to take time off from work will do it whether or not the company already has a formal leave policy in effect. Of course, sometimes this means quitting a job or eventually being subtly terminated for "other reasons." But the time for the sabbatical itself can take many different forms, whether it's created by combining vacation, sick time, personal days, and unpaid leave, or through other arrangements. Many people confuse the concept of the sabbatical as a lengthy, unbroken period of time to be used solely for self-indulgence. This isn't necessarily the case, especially since most households today require two incomes to keep them going.

A few years ago, I enrolled in a nonresidential adult degree program at Vermont College, which is part of Norwich University. Although I was still earning a living from writing at the time, I was effectively a full-time student, even though there were no such things as formal classes in the program.

This time, I was working towards my B.A. because I wanted to; my first foray into college at the age of 18 had ended after only two months. Besides, it was the middle of the recession and magazine assignments were sometimes few and far between. Sometimes weeks would go by when I did nothing but luxuriate in my studies. I'd spend one weekend a month going to meetings with my professors on campus. During the two years I was earning my degree, I truly was on sabbatical—at least some of the time.

Most of the other students in my college program held full-time jobs and had two or more kids, so they viewed their weekends spent on campus as a kind of mini-sabbatical, and after our last meeting on a Sunday afternoon, many were reluctant to leave. After all, even though we did serious work, at times it resembled one big slumber party, as it was totally unlike our ordinary day-to-day lives.

My point is that a sabbatical or family leave can be anything you want it to be in terms of length and content. Here's another example. Polly Young-Eisendrath, Ph.D., a psychologist in private practice in Philadelphia, took her sabbatical in a unique way.

Young-Eisendrath had a contract with a publisher to write a book. She estimated that it would take three months of solid writing to complete the book, but she didn't think she could take that much time away from her practice because her patients would suffer. So she decided to take one week off each month for a year.

She had previously taught in academia, and when her time for a traditional, year-long sabbatical came, Young-Eisendrath took it in order to write a scholarly book for an academic publisher. However, since she had young children at the time, it was difficult to write the book at home. "I had so many responsibilities with the children in the house that I could never turn my full attention to my writing," she said. "So I had to go away in order to write."

During her academic sabbatical year, Young-Eisendrath spent four days every month at a retreat center so that she could do nothing but write. When it came time to plan her second sabbatical, her first sabbatical served as her model.

"I knew I couldn't write the commercial book in the same way I had written the academic book, because the deadlines for the academic book weren't as hard and fast," she said.

She began her second sabbatical in September 1991. On her week off she would start by revising the chapter that she had written the month before. Then she would draft a new chapter. She completed the book a year later, working one week each month, and her book was published the following spring.

Ten Dream Sabbaticals

What follows is an admittedly biased list of what I think are the ten best ways to spend an extended period of time away from work. If none of these specifically appeals to you, make up your own list and go from there. And don't be afraid to be outrageous.

1. Build your dream house.
2. Go back to school full-time.
3. Work at a country inn for three months to see if you're cut out for it.
4. Spend two months in Italy at a cooking school.
5. Take four months off to record an album of your own compositions.
6. Intern as a hiking guide in Nepal for the summer.
7. Pursue your favorite hobby full-time as if it were your occupation.
8. Travel cross-country in an RV with no itinerary.
9. Spend six months in a house by the ocean writing the book you've always wanted to write.
10. Stay at home for a year to be a full-time parent.

Even if you know why you want time off, you're probably concerned about both the positive and negative effects that leaving work will have on your career. At this point, it's almost impossible to predict these effects, but the work you do in the next chapter will help you to become clearer about it.

2

How Time Off Will Affect Your Career

You're starting to think about taking time off, and you're even starting to fantasize about how you're planning to spend that big uninterrupted block of time, when suddenly, reality interferes:

"What will this do to my career?"

It can only harm it, you think, and so you replace thoughts of your sabbatical with the quarterly report that's due next week and the promotion that (you think) should come next year. Sadly, you start to close this book.

WAIT!

It's entirely possible that taking up to a year off from work won't affect your upward climb on the corporate ladder. It might even help you get there faster. One thing's for sure. A sabbatical won't be cause for a demotion, unless a demotion was inevitable anyway, and in that case, why would you want to continue working for a company that doesn't care whether or not its employees are happy?

Besides—and here's a hint—by the end of your sabbatical, you might find yourself rethinking absolutely everything in your life, from your career to where you live to how you spend your leisure hours. But all that comes later.

Time Off: A Career Asset

The truth is that, in most cases, taking time off from work for a sabbatical or a family leave won't hurt your career at all. You see, it takes guts and initiative to take a sabbatical if you're not a college professor, and these two qualities are sorely lacking among employees in the corporate world today. You know, you've seen them. Maybe you're even one of them. There have been so many layoffs at your company lately that although you're left behind, you're angry at the company for downsizing when there were record profits last year. So you think to yourself, "I'll show them," and put the barest minimum of your effort into your job. Maybe even less.

Or, you're surrounded by deadwood, so why should you make any effort? "No one else around here is," is your reasoning.

Even if you do possess guts and initiative, it may be that your own employer won't recognize them in you. It might take another company to appreciate all the skills you call into play when you decide to plan and then follow through with a sabbatical.

Although workers tend to hold onto their jobs when the economy is tight, the truth is that an amazing number of people change jobs every year. What's even more startling, however, is the number of men and women who totally change their careers each year: one in ten workers is the estimate.

It's no wonder, then, that in just one generation, Americans have gone from loyalist gray flannel suit types to extremely fickle butterflies, flitting from one job to another and whatever career suits them at the time—regardless of the economy. Of course, the recent workplace trends have helped to foster this sense of disloyalty, but the sheer number of people who are making a drastic change in their lives is illuminating. Many people making the switch are middle management and up who are squeezed out of their jobs in a frenzy of corporate downsizing.

Neil Bull is the director of the Center for Interim Programs in Cambridge, Massachusetts. The center focuses on helping burned-out college students take a year off—either after they graduate from high school or when they're a year or two into college—to take stock of their lives and put things into perspective. But Bull also works with corporate executives helping them design their own time off, a concept that he says will grow in corporate America. He believes that this trend will continue to parallel the major corporate trend for the nineties—how to get the most work out of the least number of warm bodies. He also thinks that those who remain behind will actually be worse off than those who are let go.

"I think it's pretty clear that people are not going to stay with the same company for thirty years the way they used to do," says Bull. "Either the company won't be there, or they'll be fired." He says that once a person has worked at a company for a number of years, she doesn't necessarily want the company to acknowledge her contribution by giving her more money; instead, she may want some breathing space. Because of this switch in worker attitudes, Bull thinks that sabbaticals are going to become commonplace in the corporate world so that businesses can hold onto valued employees. According to Bull, sabbaticals used to be seen as a reward for employees; now they're becoming a benefit, in much the same way as extended vacations and golf club memberships once were.

Can a Sabbatical Enhance Your Career?

Even though you can't see it now, any kind of time away from work will help to further your career, whether it reinforces your belief in what you're currently doing or switches you onto an entirely different career path. Some people, however, will feel less guilty about taking time off if they can somehow relate it to their work. Get your notebook and write down your responses to the following questions.

☐ Do you think your time on sabbatical would be better spent on leisure pursuits or on furthering your career?

☐ Even though you may already have a clear idea of what you want to do during your time off, come up with an idea for one sabbatical that would improve your career options, and another that would be for pure pleasure. Is there any way you can combine them?

☐ How would you list your sabbatical on your resume? Write it with a positive air.

☐ Do you want to use your sabbatical to investigate other career possibilities? If so, what are they, and how will you do it?

☐ What would you do if you knew there was no job waiting at the end of your sabbatical?

BRAINSTORM: Chart out two versions of what your resume will look like for the rest of your career—one with a sabbatical, and one without.

Professions That Make It Easy to Take a Sabbatical

Some careers are more amenable to periodic breaks than others, either because of their seasonal aspects or because most of the work is done on a project-by-project basis, with an occasional amount of downtime between them.

Of course, the higher you are in status at your company, the more your bosses will strive to make sure you're content at work. On the other hand, they may think you're so valuable to the company that they wouldn't dream of letting you go for much more than your vacation time. You may find this to be extremely flattering, but it still gets you no closer to your sabbatical.

The best candidates for taking a sabbatical are:

- [ ] Lawyers,
- [ ] Any publishing employee,
- [ ] CPAs and tax preparers,
- [ ] Teachers, and
- [ ] Secretaries and administrative assistants.

In these fields there is flexibility between projects or cases, there are naturally occurring periods of downtime, and there is usually a surplus of staff around who are competent to handle emergencies in your absence. If you're the boss of anything, you can call the shots and arrange backups any way you want. Secretaries and administrative assistants can always hire temps, a routine procedure in most offices.

The worst candidates for taking a sabbatical are:

- [ ] Anyone with a service job,
- [ ] Managers,
- [ ] Bosses, and
- [ ] Store owners.

For a low-level service job, it's usually easier to quit than to arrange a formal leave, because there are so many of these positions out there. Managers, bosses, and owners of businesses are often considered indispensable by both themselves and others, so they don't get very far in planning a sabbatical. Such indispensability is often an illusion. These positions wield a certain amount of power, and that power can be converted into developing and instituting a plan to allow for a break for the boss.

Although it's not impossible to arrange for a leave for these four worst candidates, you can still arrange for time off—albeit a shorter period of time than the five best would be able to manage—if you get creative enough, and use the guidelines in the following chapters.

Using a Sabbatical to Switch Careers

Although many career changers will do so only after the kind of enforced sabbatical that follows a massive layoff, it's much more to your advantage if you choose to take the time off to decide what you want to do next. Even if you don't quit your present job outright, testing out a different career before you switch is one of the best ways to use sabbatical time.

Here are three ways to use a sabbatical to investigate a career switch:

1. Intern or volunteer at a small business in the field of your interest. A small business means that you'll be able to see the big picture and will probably get a chance to work with the boss from time to time. At a large company, you're likely to be shuttled into one department and left to do grunt work.

2. Get a part-time job at a company in your desired field. Don't let the boss or other workers know what you're doing, but make yourself available to pitch in on a number of levels. Again, a small company is best for more complete exposure to the business.

3. If you're thinking about turning a hobby into a career or business, totally immerse yourself in it. Read the consumer

and industry publications and newsletters in the field, take some specialized workshops, read books on your subject, contact the field's trade associations, go to some conferences, in short, anything that will give you a crash course in your desired field.

Corporate Fellowships

During the years you've spent clawing your way up the corporate or other ladder, you've probably always envied the ability of academics and scholars to take their regular year-long breaks. But, of course, spending umpteen years in school to earn a doctorate never quite seemed like it was worth it to you.

Never fear. You can leapfrog right past your old psychology professor and apply for a number of fellowships that are open only to early- and mid-career men and women in all fields who've spent their formative years toiling in the corporate world.

The Luce Scholars Program (The Henry Luce Foundation, Inc., 111 West Fiftieth Street, New York, NY 10020) selects a number of men and women in their twenties each year and sends them to Asia to work for a year. The Fulbright Scholar Program (Council for the International Exchange of Scholars, 11 Dupont Circle NW, #300, Washington, DC 20036) isn't just for those who want to be president some day. Each year the program sends about 30 men and women with strong backgrounds in business all over the world to teach business or conduct research for a year. Even the White House gets into the act, offering a fellowship program to up to 20 individuals with experience in a variety of fields, where they spend a year working in some part of the executive branch (White House Fellowship Program, 1900 E Street NW, #1308, Washington, DC 20415).

The competition for these fellowships can be stiff, but if you still want one, it's a good idea to tailor your application to a program or issue that is not quite hot, but is destined to be the next big thing. For instance, try to predict what the next big reengineering of the corporation will be, and tie it into your application.

Former fellows warn that the payoff from a successful fellowship comes in the future and not during the fellowship period. Elaine Chao, a former White House fellow who left a career in banking to join the program, later served as deputy transportation secretary under George Bush, a job she wouldn't have gotten without her fellowship.

What If You Get Back and There's No Job?

Whether your company institutes layoffs in your absence—and you're an easy target—or you quit your job to take your leave—which means no safety net at the other end—the thought of nothing to return to would unnerve most people.

What to do? Relax. All of the people I interviewed for this book were able to find work when their sabbaticals were over. In fact, many of them said that their time off boosted them in the eyes of their prospective employers because it showed that they had enough initiative and strength to jump off the gerbil wheel for a time. The truth is that most careers rarely advance in a straight line and at a steady pace.

If you're determined to leave your job permanently or you find yourself returning to a discontinued position, it might benefit you to see a career counselor before your sabbatical begins to assuage your fears and help you explore ways to incorporate what you learn from your time off into creating a new job.

There are several ways to find a reputable counselor. One is to visit a temporary or permanent employment agency and gauge the demand for your area of expertise. But the problem here is that by the time you return from sabbatical, you might be in the market for a totally different kind of job, and not one that an agency counselor could easily pigeon-hole. The good thing about going to an agency counselor is you can tell him to start looking for a job for you when you're still on sabbatical, so the chances are good that you'll have a new job when you return to the real world. However, this type of counselor is usually good for only the short haul or for the long-haul, straight-and-narrow, one-career route.

If you graduated from a technical school or college, career counseling services are usually available to alumni. You can also serve as your own counselor by checking out leads on the alumni network to find out how others found their jobs, and maybe finding one for yourself in the meantime.

If you're looking to change your career, the best career counselor to have will be a person who's established in your intended career and is willing to give you advice and leads. The benefits of having such a mentor have been widely touted, although I've found that most people feel intimidated by cold calling someone who may, in essence, be their idol. I say that if you're bold enough to ask your boss for time off or to quit your job, you're pushy enough to contact a potential mentor.

Then again, it might be a good idea to forget about a safety net and decide to deal with what's next in your career when you get back. Although it may be unsettling at times, it just might end up being the best thing you've ever done.

Eight Reasons Why Employees Don't Take Sabbaticals—Even Paid Ones

1. They're afraid they'll come back to no job.
2. They think they can't afford to.

(Continued)

(Continued)

3. They think their sole rival at the company is going to leap ahead in their absence.

4. They believe the adage "out of sight, out of mind."

5. They think it will hold them back in the future when it comes to raises and promotions.

6. They don't have any idea what to do with all that free time.

7. The economy's shaky, and if they take a break, they'll be among the first to go in case of a layoff.

8. Other employees will think of them as uncommitted and disloyal, and they'll be left out of the corporate culture in the future.

Eight Reasons Why Employees Do Take Sabbaticals—With or Without Pay

1. They need a break, and a two-week vacation just won't cut it.

2. They want to spend time with their families, like in the good old days, even if it's just for a short time.

3. They want to learn a new skill, like a new language or an art form.

4. They're thinking about changing jobs.

5. They're thinking about changing careers.

6. They're thinking about starting their own businesses.

7. The company will lay them off permanently if they don't take a break. At least this way, in most cases, health insurance coverage continues, and there's the remote possibility that the employee will be called back to work.

8. They'll quit if they don't get some time away from the grind.

THE SABBATICAL FILE

Neil Bull already had been working for a couple of years helping college students plan their leaves when he was approached by the national sales manager of Merrill Lynch. The manager wanted to develop a sabbatical program for key personnel who had worked for the company for many years. "The company's intention was to reward these employees for their service and loyalty," said Bull. They began the program by working with two executives in the Seattle office, both of whom had been with the company for 30 years. Merrill Lynch wanted to use these employees as a case study for a prospective program that would eventually reach down to younger workers to help them plan their retirement. This was so that when they left the company, they wouldn't "drop dead from boredom," as Bull put it.

"Taking time off was so alien to these men that they needed me to help them plan it. Even then, it took them six months before they could get used to the idea," said Bull. "The first time I talked with one of the men and his wife, we talked for fourteen hours straight while they fantasized about some of the things that they always wanted to do."

That man was Robert Sheeran of Fall City, Washington. "As the company intended it, the purpose of my sabbatical was to go off with my wife, Betty, into a somewhat structured program that had absolutely nothing to do with my profession," he said.

After that first intensive questioning session, Bull suggested the Sheerans focus on history, since this was a shared interest of the couple. Bull then proceeded to set up a schedule where over the course of three and one half months, the Sheerans would study medieval and Viking history at Oxford, Trinity College in Ireland, and also in Sweden.

Before Sheeran took the sabbatical, the company dictated

several conditions under which the couple would be allowed to take the time off. One of them was that Sheeran would be totally divorced from his business. He was allowed to make only one phone call to the office while he was gone. "I did call once when we were at Oxford," said Sheeran, "and I ended up wishing that I had never called, because everybody dumped everything on me that had happened since I was gone. I didn't call back again."

If Bull hadn't planned his time off for him, Sheeran said that he most likely would have traveled around the world, spent a lot of money, and gotten very little out of it. "We probably would have gone off on a tangent with very little value to the time off." Sheeran, who's now retired, says that his sabbatical helped him plan his retirement. "During the leave, I had time to think about what I was going to do after I retired," he said. "I think if the people around me at the office could have taken some time off, they would have been able to sit back and ask themselves what they were going to do with the rest of their lives after they left the company. So many people treat work as the centerpiece of their lives, that when they retire, they don't have a clue about what they're going to do, so once they get there, they're absolutely lost."

Sheeran added that his time off helped to put things in perspective, and, as a result, he's become more patient. "Things that were once a big deal to me aren't now, as I see that in time, everything will take care of itself. I've also become more interested in people, and more tolerant. And because of the time we spent together, I was able to renew my relationship with my wife. On the plane coming home, I leaned over and said to her, 'Betty, if I wasn't married to you before we left, I'd certainly marry you now.'"

He said that the planning was the key to the success of his sabbatical.

"And in terms of my career, the time that I was gone was just a flick of light in the process," he added.

Future Shock

The American's Use of Time Project at the University of Maryland discovered in a 1991 survey that almost two-thirds of American workers want to have more time away from their jobs and would even trade a raise in salary for more time off. An earlier study published in 1988 by the U.S. Department of Labor also found that a significant number of people would trade salary increases for more free time, ranging from ten minutes more off of each workday to a year-long sabbatical every seven years, each with corresponding reductions in pay.

As early as 1945, a man named Albert Morton Persoff published *Sabbatical Years with Pay*. The book laid out what was and still is a revolutionary plan to reduce unemployment by giving every American worker a year off with pay every seven years. Persoff devised a convoluted plan where the productivity of workers everywhere would rise because they knew that soon it would be their turn to take a year off. He even projected that "mass unemployment," as he referred to it, would be eradicated in part by the voracious appetites of that one-seventh of the population that is always on leave. After all, writes Persoff, "A full year of leisure demands individual and social planning and facilities. . . . Our present vacation and hotel resort facilities will have to expand a thousand times to take care of the Sabbatical Year."

Although he was probably dismissed as a nut back in 1945—after all, thousands of servicepeople were just returning from the war happy to be working again, and who was Persoff to suggest a year off with all of those able-bodied heroes at hand?—it turns out that his fantasy is not terribly far-fetched. A number of companies offer paid sabbaticals to their employees about every five to ten years, and they have suffered no relative drop in productivity.

Also, when Persoff asked a sample of men and women during wartime what they would do if they could have a year off with pay and with the guarantee their jobs would be held open for them, he reported that 97 out of the 100 people he asked "had already formulated in their minds, over many years of longing and dreaming, definite and concrete plans and projects."

There's a good chance that your parents and even your grandparents knew exactly how they would have spent a year out of the grind—if they had the chance.

Now it's your turn. You can share with your relatives the disappointment of never knowing what it's like to take a month or two, or even a year, off from work, or you can take the first step. Scratch that. You've already taken the first step by buying this book. Now it's time to make your dreams a reality. Now it's time to start planning.

3

How Sabbaticals Affect Companies

You probably want to start planning your sabbatical or family leave right away. However, before you start to sock away money or plan how you're going to tell your boss, it's a good idea to know something about how sabbaticals developed in this country and be able to accurately anticipate how your own boss and company will respond when you ask for time off.

The History of Sabbaticals in the American Workplace

The idea of a sabbatical outside of academia was virtually unheard of until the 1950s, when IBM Corporation instituted its Personal Leave of Absence program. Through this program employees could take an unpaid leave of up to three months. The length of the leave was increased to one year in the 1960s and to three years in 1988.

In the past, sabbaticals also have been suggested as

management's way to deal with periodic downtimes. In the early 1960s, labor and industry organized a 13-week sabbatical for workers in the steel and aluminum industries in order to deal with sluggish times without having to lay anybody off. Although at the time the concept of sabbaticals didn't spread to other businesses, this is one way that a corporation today can still deal with a recession.

In fact, even though employees believe that taking a leave during a recession is the worst possible time to do so, the truth is that from management's standpoint, it might be the best. Economics is what spurs many corporations to look at the idea of a formal sabbatical policy in the first place.

Despite the fact that many companies say that sabbatical and family leave programs—paid or unpaid—end up costing them more than they estimate an employee's future increased productivity will bring them, a small number of corporations have adopted periodic voluntary sabbatical programs to help cut costs in downtimes without having to permanently lay off employees. AT&T instituted a program called the Special Enhanced Leave of Absence (SELOA) to take advantage of slow times, and at the same time give a break to those employees at management level or higher who want it. The leave is unpaid but all benefits continue, and a job is guaranteed upon the employee's return. The employee must have five years or more of service to the company to qualify. An unusual twist on the SELOA program is that the leaves can only be for a minimum of nine months and a maximum of two years. AT&T also offers employees on leave up to $8,000 for tuition assistance for each year of the leave. Since the program began in 1991, more than 1,600 workers out of the 90,000 who are eligible have taken a leave, with the average leave lasting 15 months.

Even though the program is generous, AT&T's payout is far less than what it would cost the company to have the worker on payroll for a full year.

IBM originally began its Personal Leave of Absence program in the 1950s, and over the years it has undergone several modifications. In 1988 the policy of the program was changed to include unpaid leaves for up to three years while benefits continued, along with guaranteed job placement upon the employee's return. The policy also states that an employee may be called back for part-time work during the second and/or third years of a leave. Back in the mid 1980s, the company granted leaves to almost any employee who requested one. Today, however, it's a different story, because for the last several years the company has been laying off thousands of workers. Although it's likely that IBM management would grant a request for a leave, there's also a good chance that after a leave an employee would not be able to find work with the company again.

Anticipating Your Company's Response

Even though you think you know your boss, in most cases it's impossible to predict precisely how she'll react to your request for time off. And even if you think you know, it may still surprise you.

It never hurts to do your homework and get a sense of how the company has treated other employees who have taken leaves in the past. Write your answers to the following questions in your notebook.

1. How do you think your boss will respond when you ask for time off?

2. Has the company ever granted a leave to an employee? Can you find out the specifics? How was the company approached, how long was the leave, and what was its purpose? Also, at what level was the employee?

3. Can you locate an employee who applied for a leave and was turned down? Again, find out the details. If the employee has since quit, try to track him down.

4. Does your company have a soft spot? If you plan to take time off to help a good cause, can you somehow make it jibe with the company's charitable interests?

THE SABBATICAL FILE

Ray Daniels of Boulder, Colorado, had been working as the manager of a federal systems company at IBM when he took advantage of the Personal Leave of Absence program in 1993. "My job was very stressful, and my health began to suffer," he said.

He originally planned to stay out for one year, but he found that shortly after he began his leave, he was hesitant about going back, in part because of the company's guaranteed job policy. "I knew that I couldn't take a sabbatical without losing something, because when I went back I knew I'd have to take any job they told me to take," he said.

When he first applied for his leave, Daniels said, IBM was approving anyone who wanted to go. As a manager, he'd seen people above and below him on the corporate ladder take leaves, and he'd even helped to approve other employees for their leaves. "We always considered the needs of the business against the request," he said. "And in past years, when we had a surplus of manpower, it became almost routine to grant a leave for any reason." The company has since tightened up its policy.

But when Daniels wanted to take his leave, the company initially didn't want to approve it. "Usually when someone in the management chain leaves, it opens a hole and creates anxiety among the staff. They wanted me to continue going up the ladder and stay on the track, and in the end the whole thing turned out to be about doing something that's right for me instead of for the company," he said. The company's fears were justified, however, because their past experience with the leave program had shown that the more senior level the position of the leavetaker, the more unlikely it was that the employee would return from the leave.

Daniels spent the first three months of his sabbatical detoxifying—as he put it—from the 60-hour workweeks and from having much of his personal identity tied up in his job. "It took a long time before I was ready to let go of that," he said.

After he detoxified, Daniels spent time bicycling, playing tennis, doing volunteer work, and thinking about what he really wanted to do for work. "Before I took my sabbatical, I knew that I would spend part of my time off thinking about what I really wanted to be doing. My job sucked so much out of me that I never had the time to decide what I wanted to do," he said. "I knew I needed to get out so I could create the time to think." He began to do some market research on a variety of business ideas that he thought he'd like to start. He went to a few trade shows and kicked around some ideas with friends.

Nine months into his leave, IBM offered its employees an early retirement option, and Daniels grabbed it in order to start a new business.

Progressive Computer Companies Help Shape Sabbatical Policy

Perhaps the most famous boss in recent years to take a sabbatical was John Sculley, former CEO of Apple Computers. The company has had a sabbatical policy in effect since 1985, specifying that every employee could take a six-week paid leave from the company after five full years of service. In 1988, when Sculley became eligible, he decided to take off.

Tacking three weeks of vacation time on to his sabbatical, Sculley spent most of his leave in Maine, where he took a photography workshop, designed a barn for his ranch in California, and began planning a revamp of the entire company. Even though he spent an hour on the business for each day of his sabbatical, he returned to work rejuvenated.

Sculley believes that the computer industry is ideally suited to offer regular sabbatical programs. "Things move at such a fast pace," he said in a 1989 magazine article.[1] "You have to pour yourself into what you're doing. It's very useful to be able to pull back, catch your breath, and try to gain some perspective."

Which is just what he did on his time off.

Besides law firms, companies on the West Coast, and in California's Silicon Valley in particular, seem more likely to make sabbaticals available as a standard employee benefit. Young, high-tech companies in the area are more people oriented and progressive, and so are more likely to offer sabbaticals to their employees; these businesses really want to hang onto their talent. The competition among these companies has gotten intense, which is best demonstrated by the true-more-often-than-not myth of the employee who just walks across the street to get a little more money, although the recession has slowed things down a bit.

Tandem, a software company in Cupertino, California, offers every employee six weeks off with pay four years after being hired. And every subsequent four years, the employee gets another six weeks off. Tom Waldrop, who works in the public communications department at Tandem, has taken three sabbaticals since he's started with the company. He took the first to go trekking in Nepal, spent the second at home taking it easy, and on the third, traveled with his wife and infant throughout the Pacific Northwest. He says that his pattern is typical for people at the company: On the first sabbatical, he took the trip he always dreamed of and came back exhausted. On the second, he did the complete opposite—stayed home and did nothing—and was bored stiff. On

[1]O'Reilly, Brian. "John Sculley on Sabbatical." *Fortune* 119 (March 27, 1989): 79–80.

the third, he was able to strike a balance between travel and relaxation.

"Taking a sabbatical means change, whether you come back to the same job or not," says Waldrop, whose job was changed by management after he came back from his first sabbatical. "It means you're replaceable since other people can do your work and you have to help out. It taught me a lesson that no one is unexpendable, and that working on a team means you have to accept the idea that you can walk away for a while. I think one reason we all stay on the treadmill of work is that this way, it's easier to be reassured of your value to the company. When I went away, I wondered if I would still be recognized for what I do."

He and other employees at Tandem also have acknowledged that part of the reason they take a sabbatical is to recommit themselves to what they're doing at the company. "Going away has given me a chance to think, 'Do I want to continue to work for this company and do this job?' For this reason, for both the company and the employees, this is a major benefit of taking a sabbatical."

Waldrop also recognizes the quirkiness of working for a company where everyone who's there longer than four years takes a break. "There's definitely an adjustment period for everyone, and people almost joke about it. I was talking to a guy the other day who told me it was his first day back from sabbatical. He said he wasn't sure who he was, and that he had to look at the name on the door to his office to check. The rule of thumb is if you come back and feel very disoriented, then the odds are that you had a good sabbatical, because it means you've really let go, and it will take some time to turn your focus back onto work. In fact, discussing sabbaticals is part of the culture here," he says. "It's a real ritual."

Kevin Kean, group manager of product management at Tandem, spent his eight-week sabbatical in the spring of 1992 traveling with his wife through Europe. By the time he returned to work, he had reached a level that he calls the optimum mix of stress and enjoyment. The first two weeks that he was away, he thought about his job occasionally and remained connected to the office in his mind. But he continued to relax. As the sabbatical progressed, he says he became more and more disconnected from his work. He reached a plateau of relaxation after the third week of his trip. "By the time the eight weeks were over," he said, "I was completely disconnected, and came back to work a clean slate. I was ready to start my job all over again."

This is what companies that offer sabbaticals as a regular benefit count on.

According to a Conference Board report on sabbaticals,[2] Genentech, Inc., a biotechnology company, believes that the enhanced retention rate is the major benefit that sabbaticals provide for a company. Genentech statistics show that after the sabbatical program began, employees stopped quitting in droves after their third or fourth year of employment, which is what previously had happened.

Among companies that most often offer sabbaticals as a benefit to their employees, law firms appear to be the most generous. Unlike Martha Owens, the legal administrator in chapter 1, many in that profession don't have much trouble convincing the boss, because many law firms do offer their partners regular paid sabbaticals. John Kulewicz, an attorney with the firm of Vorys, Sater, Seymour and Pease, in Columbus, Ohio, took a company-sanctioned sabbatical of three months in 1991, which is offered to partners after ten years of service to the firm and again every five years afterwards. One of the founding partners started the program in

[2]Axel, Helen. *Redefining Corporate Sabbaticals for the 1990s*. New York: The Conference Board, 1992.

1968 as a way to retain good employees and to also provide a big boost to the morale within the organization. "People often leave a company because they're looking for an opportunity to get away for a while to spend time with their families or to do something different," says Kulewicz. He adds that offering periodic leaves certainly helps to retain employees. "It can also enhance the development of a business in terms of the things an employee learns about while she's gone, especially if she goes overseas to a different culture or economy."

Kulewicz, who used to serve on the hiring committee for new attorneys, says that when the sabbatical benefit was mentioned to prospective employees, the perk had a lot of appeal. "Law firms are more amenable to offering sabbaticals perhaps because this is a profession and not an assembly line," he adds. The program at his firm is only offered to partners, and Kulewicz says that others have used the program to take long family vacations, to travel, and to learn to play golf. Some partners have even gone to work for companies that are clients of the firm. A few partners haven't come back from their sabbaticals because they ended up working for the other business.

"There's a guy who's been here long enough to have taken several sabbaticals with his family. His kids are grown now, but they look back at the sabbaticals as the most special time they can remember with their family," says Kulewicz.

Although most of the partners at the firm think that the sabbatical program is a great opportunity, surprisingly enough, not all take advantage of it. "Half the lawyers take it regularly, a quarter take the time off on an occasional basis, while another quarter of the partners don't take it at all," says Kulewicz. Although many of the partners take their sabbaticals in summer in order to spend time with their families, it's the firm's priority to make sure that pressing business is taken care of before a partner takes a leave. "I'm sure that if everybody wanted to take a sabbatical at the same time, we'd have to stagger it somewhat."

How One Company Does It

Typically, the employees who can easily arrange to take leaves in companies that don't offer formal leave policies are likely to be in the upper echelons of management. This is not only because the company naturally places more value on an executive than on a secretary or clerk, but also because these workers are more likely to be able to afford an extended period of time off. The longer the leave, the more likely it is to be without pay, however, in most cases, an employee's benefits will continue. But at some companies, anyone is eligible to take time off, regardless of his or her level.

Employees at Wells Fargo Bank of San Francisco who want to take special leaves are required to qualify under one of the bank's two leave programs: The Personal Growth Leave and the Social Service Leave. The Personal Growth Leave is for employees who've been with the bank ten or more years and wish to pursue an activity of their choice for up to three months. The Social Service Leave provides employees with the opportunity to delve into a project with a nonprofit organization for up to six months; their tenure at the company needs to be three years in length. Both kinds of leaves provide the employee with full salary and continued benefits. Wells Fargo began the leave programs in 1976, following the lead of Xerox, which a few years earlier had put together a leave program that received a lot of attention.

According to Tim Hanlon, a vice president who administers the leaves, commitment to a goal is the first thing that he and the committee of up to nine high-level employees look for in an applicant for a Personal Growth Leave. This helps to narrow the pool of applicants, since up to sixty employees may apply each year for what averages out to seven leaves, based on an aggregate number of months allowed by the bank. "A lot of people would like to take time off, but they don't take the time to think through what they would like to do with a leave," he says. Of the seven leaves granted in 1993, one employee took time off to help her brother, who had been in jail, earn a GED. Another began to record an album of original music.

Some of the Wells Fargo leaves start immediately after permission is granted; others begin later on in the year. The bank requires that the leave be completed within that calendar year, but the final decision on whether an employee can take a leave—and when—still comes down to the departmental manager.

"The company grants the leave, but it's very important that the leavetaker's manager be on board with the program, or else there's trouble," says Hanlon. "After all, the people who are going to suffer the most are the employees in the department where the leavetaker works. The manager will need to hire and train a temporary employee and manage to do without the regular colleague, so it's important that the manager and co-workers are involved in the program throughout the process. Wells Fargo softens the blow even more by transferring the employee on leave to my department, which pays his salary along with all benefits so that the department isn't taking a double hit," he says.

Dave Kvederis, a senior vice-president in commercial banking sales at Wells Fargo, took a three-month Social Service Leave in the summer of 1993 to go to Lithuania and work on several projects designed to modernize the country's financial system. He worked through the U.S. Treasury as a banking advisor to the Lithuanian government. He made contact through a program administered by the Federal Reserve, which allocates money to a special fund that provides assistance to help emerging countries adjust to a free-market economy. Kvederis spent his leave in Vilnius, the capital, working on a variety of projects, including privatizing the largest consumer bank in the country and introducing a new national currency.

"I got to work on things that I'll never get a chance to do in the United States," says Kvederis, a second-generation Lithuanian. The Federal Reserve was already familiar with his work through Wells Fargo, and they also knew he was fluent in the language. Through networking, contacts, and the Social Service Leave, he was able to arrange his time off.

Evelyn McClure, of Sebastopol, California, also worked for Wells Fargo. She took a Personal Growth Leave for one month in 1990 to work on and complete a portfolio of her photographs in order to earn a fine arts certificate in photography. She had worked for the company for ten years, and she applied because she wanted to pursue photography in more depth than the hobby it was at the time.

During her month off, she spent a lot of time in her darkroom, shot a couple of projects, and finished her portfolio. She returned to her job and worked for the bank for a few more years when she took her second, albeit unofficial, sabbatical by quitting. "My first leave gave me a taste of what it was like to have time off, and so I decided to do it again, only on my terms," said McClure.

The Hidden Costs to Corporations

Both employers and employees benefit from sabbaticals, but the real harm from a company's lack of a sabbatical policy may be hidden. If employees see that they have absolutely no options within the corporation—which includes a company's reluctance to grant time off, even unpaid—they may eventually decide to leave and find a company that can provide them with this flexibility. Out walks one of the company's biggest investments.

The Real Costs to Corporations

Whether an employee takes a leave as sanctioned by the Family Medical Leave Act or wants to take six months to study Italian in Venice, there is the cost to the company to consider. This cost includes hiring a temporary replacement, staggering the workload among other employees, or letting the work go undone. Sometimes the price is high, particularly to smaller companies.

Although many companies are rightfully concerned about the costs of hiring a temporary replacement for the leave taker, at least one large corporation discovered that this was not a major concern. In 1989 the Du Pont Company increased the length of its family leave program from two to six months and also expanded the program to include fathers of newborns. Since they instituted the changes, more than 1,000 employees have taken a leave. But an informal survey of these employees showed that only seven percent had replacements while they were gone, which is far below what most managers expect.

4

Planning Your Time Off

Sitting down in advance to plan a sabbatical or family leave is a little like planning a marriage: You have certain expectations about what it will be like, and you fantasize about the good parts while totally negating the bad parts.

How can you plan for something that you've never experienced? Like everything in life, you won't really know what it will be like until you're in the thick of it. But there is a certain amount of structuring you can do in advance to make sure your time off will be fruitful and match your expectations. Although some people do take time off to do nothing more than be with their children, these types of leaves tend to be shorter—about six to eight weeks. But even if spending more time with your kids is one thing you want from your sabbatical, there are probably other things you'll also want to accomplish over the course of your leave.

Most people allow finances to serve as their excuse when they say they'd like to take time off. "I'd love it," they say, "but I really can't afford it." Solving your financial problems is usually the easiest part of the sabbatical-planning process. (See chapter 5). However, when the choices boil down to what you really want to do, it's always possible to find a way to do it without requiring too much money. Your time off may involve a paying job, but such a job will probably be very different from what you've been doing.

What causes more headaches is making sure that everything comes together at the same time. You see, planning for a sabbatical involves mostly logistics: what you're going to do, where you're going to be, how you're going to deal with your house or apartment while you're gone, what you're going to do with your job, and how you're going to pay for it all. Doing your homework from the beginning can help alleviate the fear—no, the terror—that many people feel once the safety net of their job has been yanked out from under them.

The idea of what you're going to do has usually been marinating for years, perhaps a lifetime. The first thing to do is to narrow your scope and then hone in on one particular aspect of what it is you want to do.

What Do You Want to Do?

When planning your sabbatical, first decide exactly how you'd like to spend it and build in some flexibility. "Getting people to uncover what they really want to be doing on sabbatical is like working on a jigsaw puzzle," says Nella Barkley, co-founder of the Crystal-Barkley Corporation in New York, a firm that provides guidance for career and life changes. "The first pieces that appear don't really make much sense in the beginning, but later when they start to fill in the pieces, more of the picture starts to emerge." Barkley first directs her clients to identify the things they most want to do with their lives, which often are those things they used to dream about when they were younger and which, unfortunately, have been suppressed over the years.

I was surprised to discover that many people don't have a clear idea of how they'd like to spend an extended leave. It may sound easy, but deciding what you want to do with a chunk of time that doesn't have to be spent working can be rather difficult. Some people might automatically respond by saying they want to travel around the world, but that frequently tends to be just a stock answer. When they dig a little deeper, they see that perhaps they'd want to travel to Italy or Turkey, and maybe pursue a lifelong interest in archaeology.

"It's very difficult for people to know exactly what it is they want to do, because their real desires have been so submerged after years of being and acting the way that other people expect them to be," Barkley says.

Neil Bull of the Center for Interim Programs agrees. "I don't think that most people know what they want; because if they know what they want to do, they just go ahead and do it," he says. He points to teachers at all levels—from elementary school to high school, many of whom receive the opportunity to take a sabbatical as a matter of course—as being particularly unimaginative when it comes to deciding how they're going to spend their time off. "Most of them end up going to Maine to write The Book," says Bull. "But there are so many other things a person could do to get out of her current value system and also recharge her battery, that it's worth taking a look at all of her options.

"No one has ever walked in here and said, 'I want to learn how to raise sled dogs with Susan Butcher up in Alaska,' and yet we've had a continuous group of people going up there for a number of years," he adds. "It isn't until I dump it in their laps that they see that it's a perfect opportunity for them."

Your Sabbatical Plan

If you haven't yet narrowed down exactly what you want to do, or if you can't decide between several of your ideas, then write out a sabbatical plan for each of them. Seeing the specifics down in black and white may just help you to make your final decision. Once you do start to narrow down what you want to do, it's a good idea to have all of the broad strokes confirmed so you can start planning the details that will make up your sabbatical. To begin, get out your notebook and ask yourself the following questions. Keep in mind that some of your answers will become more refined as you read on in the book.

- ☐ How am I going to spend my sabbatical? Be as specific as possible.
- ☐ How long do I think I'll need?
- ☐ Am I going to stay in one place—either at home or somewhere else—or travel around? And where do I want to go?
- ☐ When do I want it to start?
- ☐ How much time do I need to plan?
- ☐ What can my friends and family help me with?
- ☐ How much money do I need to save?
- ☐ How long can I feasibly be away from work?
- ☐ Should my sabbatical have a definite end, or be open-ended?
- ☐ Do I want to spend my time doing nothing?

BRAINSTORM:

- [ ] Pick a target date when you're going to start your sabbatical. This will give you something concrete to work towards.

- [ ] Take your list of 25 things from Chapter One and narrow them down to 10. Could some of them be combined?

How Much Time Do You Need?

Benchmarks like a year, six months, or three months are mentioned as ideal lengths for a sabbatical because they're nice round numbers, but more importantly, it's easier to get corporations to agree to them, unless you have a specific project in mind that will take exactly five-and-a-half months. Even so, it's a good idea to build in a little downtime on both sides of a sabbatical so that before you go you are able to prepare and focus on what you want to accomplish, and on the downside so you can decompress a little and be ready to return to the working world.

But deciding how much time you're going to need is not an exact science. It depends entirely on the individual. Some people plan for three months when they would benefit more from six months, while others who take a year find that they're ready to go back to work after only six months. The amount of time you need to plan your leave depends on you and your financial situation (see chapter 5). If you need to plan every little detail in order to feel confident enough to leave your job, then take up to a year or more to plan it. But if you believe that the longer you put it off, the more likely your sabbatical will remain just a good idea, then by all means, do whatever is necessary to get your affairs in order and plunge right in, perhaps only after a couple of months of planning.

A good rule of thumb is to allow one month to plan for each month that you'll be away, but this isn't carved in stone. Some people who have formal sabbatical policies at their office need only to plan travel, since their salaries will continue. On the whole, though, traveling sabbaticals do need more advance planning: Some people start planning a year in advance for a six-week travel sabbatical. However, if you decided only yesterday to begin your leave next week, you'll need to condense the following guidelines.

How Much Time Do You Need to Plan Your Time Off?

First, set the date. Then:

12 months in advance: Determine how long your leave will be. Send away for brochures about programs you want to attend and places you want to visit. Start saving money and cutting your expenses.

10 months in advance: Get all your questions answered from the different sources you're investigating.

8 months in advance: Start negotiating with your boss. It might help to set your target date during a slow time at the office. Present your proposal (see chapter 6). Be prepared for an argument and to defend your choice for a leave.

6 months in advance: Finalize your plans. Make sure all applications, deposits, and reservations are in. Keep socking money away.

4 months in advance: Start to purchase the special items you'll need for your sabbatical.

3 months in advance: If you're leaving home, decide what you're going to do about your home while you're away. Start advertising for tenants and figure out where you're going to store your possessions, if necessary. Start to draw up a

(Continued)

(Continued)

list of the goals you plan to reach during and after your sabbatical.

2 months in advance: If you're going away, make sure that the person who's handling your financial and legal situations is well versed in what he needs to do (see chapter 5). Continue to save money.

1 month in advance: Make a checklist of everything you still need for your sabbatical, and buy it now. Double-check that your tenants are still planning to move in on the agreed date.

2 weeks in advance: Make sure that everything's set for you to begin your sabbatical as planned.

1 week in advance: Start packing.

The day before: Drop off the dog, check that your car is working, confirm your reservations, and when you leave the office, don't look back.

Do Your Homework

Overall, no matter how people decide they want to spend their time off, the amount of research they do is quite critical to whether or not the sabbatical ever takes place—in most cases. Some people actually do better with their sabbatical if they do a minimal amount of planning. (See the How Not to Plan section later in this chapter.)

For the planners, though, once they've researched and planned what they're going to do, they also discover that they do indeed have the courage to go ahead with their plans. Many people check out absolutely everything, from the geographic location, if they're going to travel or live elsewhere for a while, to meeting with people who have taken leaves before. This guarantees them an established network of supportive people before they even set foot outside the office.

THE SABBATICAL FILE

Ben Strohecker, CEO and founder of Harbor Sweets, a luxury chocolate company in Salem, Massachusetts, took the year 1989 off in order to reach two very specific goals. "Half of it was to prove to the management group at the company that they could run the business very nicely without me should I ever get hit by a truck," he said. "The other half was that I always wanted to devote a year to public service."

That service was to increase the awareness of CEOs to the effects of AIDS in the workplace. A couple of years before he took his sabbatical, Strohecker had attended a seminar on AIDS in the workforce. The sponsoring agency had sent 3,000 letters to CEOs and human resource people on the north shore of Massachusetts, but Strohecker was the only CEO to show up.

"I didn't know anyone who had AIDS, but after the seminar I felt that I should approach other people like me, and I began trying to raise funds. My destiny was to be speaking to business groups," he said.

After he began his sabbatical, he was invited to talk about AIDS with area Episcopal churches, as well as several national organizations. One of them, the National Coalition on AIDS, asked him if he would work as a loaned executive out of Washington both addressing different business groups and being on call to talk with them about AIDS. When the coalition got a call from a trade organization saying that one of their employees had AIDS—which Strohecker says was almost always a panic call—they would send him to talk with and calm the top executives at the company. During his year off he traveled all over the country.

Doing Good: Four Considerations

Whether you want to spend your leave working as a missionary in Mexico or as a volunteer in the AIDS ward of your local hospital, there are certain things you should take into account before you sign up to spend the next year giving of yourself.

1. Be very clear why you want to do this. People either are benevolent towards each other or they are not. Signing up to do a tour of duty in a teen center in the inner city just because it makes you look good will quickly backfire. You'll be there for the wrong reasons, the staff and other volunteers will pick up on it, and before long they'll probably ask you to leave. Then you're left with a number of months remaining on your leave with nothing to do except sheepishly return to work.

2. If you're going to commit to a particular agency for an extended period of time, give it a trial period at first. Admittedly, although they probably are in dire need of volunteers, the people who run a soup kitchen will be more likely to agree to your request to work full-time for a couple of months writing grants and contacting local restaurants for donations if they're already familiar with the kind of work you can do.

Start out by volunteering a couple of nights or one day a week. You'll get a feel for the intricacies of the place and at the same time regular staffers will be able to get an idea of how you work and even may suggest another department for you where the match would be a better one.

3. Don't be afraid to back out if you think you can't handle it. Being a full-time volunteer in a selfish society may be difficult for you and your ego to take. And you shouldn't expect the people around you to welcome you with open arms because you've decided to give of yourself and your time. There are too many fires for them to put out to spend any time stroking your ego. Besides, you're there to work, and that's all that matters. They know that, so expect to hit the ground running.

4. If you are getting paid by the nonprofit organization

you've chosen, you might be able to convince your company to donate your salary to it during your sabbatical. It would be a tax deduction, and your company could get some favorable publicity, both locally and in the trade, for its actions. In fact, if your boss is still reluctant to let you go, this might just be the bargaining chip that changes her mind—especially if you present your plan to your company's donation department at the same time you tell your boss.

The 10 Best Sabbaticals for Volunteer Work

1. Volunteer at your local humane society or animal league society.

2. Spend a summer with Habitat for Humanity, building houses for low-income families in your area. For more information, contact Habitat for Humanity International, 121 Habitat Street, Americus, GA 31709-3498.

3. Work the phones at a suicide prevention hotline. After your sabbatical ends, you can continue one shift a week.

4. Become a volunteer at your local hospital.

5. Start your own walkathon, collecting pledges for the cause of your choice, and then take an extended walk across your state or the entire country.

6. Help the American Hiking Society or Appalachian Mountain Club clean up existing trails on their network or build new ones.

7. Join the Peace Corps for a year. Write Peace Corps, Washington, DC 20526.

8. Work on a project with Earthwatch, a group that matches volunteers with scientists and other researchers who are conducting investigations and experiments all over the world. Write Earthwatch, 680 Mount Auburn Street, Box 403, Watertown, MA 02272.

(Continued)

(Continued)

9. Work on a community service project in the country of your choice under the auspices of Volunteers for Peace, an organization that runs more than a thousand such work camps throughout Europe and Africa. Write Volunteers For Peace, Tiffany Road, Belmont VT 05730.

10. Live and work on an organic farm in the United States or overseas. Contact Willing Workers on Organic Farms, Mt. Murrindal Coop, Buchan, Victoria 3885, Australia.

THE SABBATICAL FILE

It's difficult enough to plan for a sabbatical when you haven't done it before, but what happens when a whole family decides to take a year off? Does the planning get exponentially more difficult?

Not always. Actually, it can be a lot easier. Back in 1988, Jane and Tom Babbitt of Camden, Maine, were ready for an adventure. Tom's company was going through a transition, and he saw that he already had gone as far as he could in his position as senior vice president. He simply didn't have the challenges that he once had.

Jane worked as a volunteer and spent most of her time at home as mother to their two daughters, Laura, who was seven at the time, and Mary, who was ten and not yet into adolescence, "which requires that a telephone be constantly affixed to her ear," as Jane put it. The girls were both old enough to understand everything that was going on and were willing to leave their friends for a year. The stage was set.

Jane had been sailing since she was five years old; Tom began sailing when he was twelve. "He lives to sail," said Jane. Every fall, from their outpost on the Atlantic Ocean, the Babbitts would watch the boats head south for the winter and think, "If only we could do that."

These are always prophetic words. In the Babbitts' case, they led to a year-long sabbatical on a 40-foot boat sailing from Maine to Florida and on to the Caribbean before the family headed back up to Maine. Since the girls would be out of school for the year, Jane and Tom arranged for correspondence courses through the Calvert School of Baltimore, which provided Laura and Mary with lesson plans, pens, pencils, workbooks, and prepaid mailers so they could send the completed work back to the school for grading. At their next scheduled port, the tests would be waiting for the Babbitts to pick up.

"It was like following a flight plan, since someone knew where we were all the time," Jane said. Working out the arrangements with their local post office to forward mail to certain addresses at particular times was the easy part. "Overall, planning for the sabbatical was difficult because we didn't know what to anticipate, because there wasn't enough written about how to do everything. So we figured a lot of it out ourselves. We went through all of our household items and asked what was absolutely necessary for us to take. It turned out not to be much, since storage space on the boat was limited. We basically took only clothing and books."

The Babbitts also packed up everything except their furniture and stored it in their garage before they rented out their house. Jane arranged with their local newspaper to write an occasional article about their trip so that their friends and the town could stay posted on what they were doing. As it turned out, Jane is very glad she did this.

"When we got back, I didn't have to explain why the family had been missing for more than a year. Everyone already knew."

School Days

If you plan to take your whole family on a sabbatical during the school year, it's important to arrange in advance to make sure your school-aged kids keep up with their schoolwork so they don't fall behind.

There are two ways you can do this. First, contact the principal where your child attends school. Explain why you're taking your child out of school and what you'll be doing. Tell the principal that you want to keep current with lessons, and ask if your child's teacher can prepare a packet of lessons in advance. Or, after explaining your plans to the principal, obtain lessons from one of the schools offering correspondence courses for kids in kindergarten through twelfth grade. This option will endear you in the eyes of your child's teacher, since it will save her from a lot of extra work. Here are the names and addresses of two such schools: The Calvert School, 105 Tuscany Road, Baltimore, MD 21210 and the American School, 850 East Fifty-eighth Street, Chicago, IL 60637.

Of course, the school can't prevent you from taking your kids out of classes for a while, but you'll earn brownie points if you show that you're willing to work with the school. It helps if either you or your spouse is a teacher, but barring that, use one of the correspondence courses that are used widely by children who aren't based at one particular school.

And when they return to school, your kids will have great material for Show and Tell.

You First

It just so happens that both you and your spouse think that taking a sabbatical is a wonderful idea, but only one of you can afford to take off at a time. What can you do?

When Debra Phillips planned to take her sabbatical so that she could go away to school, she had an agreement with her husband that after she returned to work, it would be his turn to take time off from his job. He also wanted to go back to school to work on a graduate degree in history at a nearby university. He supported her while she was gone, and when his turn came to take time off, she worked both to support him and also to pay off the debts she had incurred while on her sabbatical. During both of their sabbaticals, however, they each began to evaluate their marriage and where they wanted to go with it.

"My time off was very helpful to me in figuring out where I wanted to go in this marriage," she said. Her husband would visit her occasionally, and she also flew home about once a month to see him. She says that being on their own resurrected an independence that had faded away for both of them during the twelve years they were married. "The sabbatical was such a wonderful clearing-out process for me, that I was able to see what was important to me in my life. As a result, I began to create some degree of balance in my life." When she came back, this awareness spilled over into the relationship with her husband, and they began to see a marriage counselor. "I came back and asked, 'Where are we going with this marriage, and what are our goals?' As a result, we discovered that we have very different goals, from both a personal and professional standpoint."

Although they stayed together for both of their sabbatical years, they realized that the relationship was ending, and between her new job and his schooling, there was an enormous grieving process going on in the background. Yet, if they hadn't had each other, their sabbaticals would have been impossible.

How to Get an Internship

If you want to spend your sabbatical interning, the odds are that you won't have to compete with high school and college students for a position. Instead, you'll have to design your own plan for finding a position using cold calls or contacting friends of friends, or through admiring the work, say, of a newspaper, telling the owner that you'd love to learn the business, and you just happen to have the next three months free and it looks like he could use some help.

You'll probably have more opportunities to intern open to you at any time of the year except for summer, because you won't have to compete with large numbers of young students who view an internship as an integral part of going to college.

You, on the other hand, have other reasons for interning, and even though you may raise a few eyebrows when you announce that you're looking to intern, the fact is that many businesses regularly use interns. They will probably not be that picky should someone a little or a lot older and with a lot more experience than the typical intern want to apply for a position.

True, for a business, many internships are no more than a way to get the grunt work done, which doesn't seem to bother the myriad warm bodies that are grateful to get a peek at the inner workings of what they view as a glamour business. Age and experience, however, are on your side should you land an internship at a prestigious company. For one thing, although you're there to learn, you probably won't be as wide-eyed as the young coeds who would usually fill your seat, and you're better able to notice the nuances of the business since you're already familiar with how an office operates. For another, since it's difficult for an adult to be content with grunt work, you'll probably ask more questions and request more interesting work to do in addition to the normal amount of work that will be ready and waiting for you the first day of your internship. Also, because you're an adult, your supervisor will be more inclined to give you more interesting assignments.

If you opt for an internship, make the most of it, whether

you're there for one month or longer. No matter what your age, an internship is still a valuable way to see the inner workings of a particular field before you decide whether it's for you.

Planning Your Travel

A good travel agent who is familiar with your likes and dislikes is almost indispensable these days. But if you want something more exotic, you might have to do your planning alone. For instance, if you want to spend six weeks trekking through Nepal, which seems to be one of the most popular sabbatical choices today, you need to go through a specialized outfitter that is licensed to lead groups in that country. Check the back pages of *Outside* and *Backpacker* magazines for ads for companies that arrange group travel in Nepal.

If you want to be self-directed, there are some countries where, as of this writing, you have to travel with government-sanctioned guides. China is still one such destination. Again, if you contact travel companies that specialize in arranging these kinds of trips, you'll be better off than going through your own travel agent.

Most people who are adventurous enough to take a sabbatical aren't willing to settle for the garden-variety group tours geared to people who want to know in advance what to expect from their trips. Whether you're traveling cross-country in your car without a map or backpacking through Europe and don't know where you're going to stay each night, there's plenty of information available to help you.

The Lonely Planet guidebook series not only tells you how to travel in countries like Thailand and Poland and what to bring, it also gives you a rudimentary education about local customs and etiquette. It will tell you how much to budget for expenses and the best ways to travel around the country.

If you decide to camp out in the United States, it's worth it to join one of the national organizations like the American Camping Association or the Good Sam Parks. They will provide you with information about thousands of parks and campgrounds nationwide and give you member discounts on hookup rates. If you've never been camping before, or have dim memories of it from childhood, don't be afraid to ask whatever you will. To these associations, there's no such thing as a dumb question.

If you plan to stay in one place for all of your sabbatical, it might be worth your while to look into the possibility of exchanging your house or apartment with someone who has a residence in the area you've selected. There are several home exchange organizations that for a fee match up appropriate swappers. Or, you can check out the ads in alumni publications for academics who frequently trade houses for a summer or their sabbatical year. Obviously, if you live in a desirable area, it will be easier to find someone to trade with. With a home exchange, you are responsible both for paying the rent or mortgage on your own home and covering the utilities in your guest house while you're away.

Taking Care of Your House While You're Gone

If you're leaving your house to travel around the world or just to stay somewhere else for a workshop or course, you'll do many of the same things that you regularly do when you leave on a two-week vacation; some of them, however, will require more detail.

If your house or apartment will be vacant, it's a good idea to stop mail and newspaper delivery and arrange for a friend or a top-rate kennel to care for your pets if you can't take them with you. The same security rules apply—lights on timers, a neighbor's car parked in the driveway from time to time, etc.—but if you can afford it, hiring a reputable bonded house sitter who will visit the house, water the plants, feed the fish, walk the dog, and take in the mail and paper is worth the $15–$30 each day it will cost, depending on where you live. You can hire an individual sitter who you may elect to actually live in your house instead of just visit it each day, or go through a house-sitting agency, where the managers have already done all the screening for you.

Other things you can do to protect your house while you're away are to make sure the lawn is cut and watered regularly and the walks are swept and kept clear of snow.

Have the person who is handling your finances pay the utility bills each month from your checking account, or else contact the utility companies and send them a check for the estimated amount that will be used while you're away. Then, if you're renting out the house, arrange to be reimbursed by your tenant, or build a surplus to cover it.

How Not to Plan

What if you don't have any big plans for your sabbatical? What if you want to start off by reading and relaxing, and you know the ideas will follow once you've removed yourself from the structured work routine?

Some people, undoubtedly, will benefit from a lack of structure. If they think about it too much, they'll end up talking themselves out of it. Others simply don't have the time to plan, and once the time for their sabbatical arrives, that's when they decide what to do. This method isn't for the fainthearted, especially if it involves international travel, but sometimes it turns out to be the most important part of the sabbatical.

Some people like to start off their leave by going the opposite route of their jobs: no schedules, no routine, no have-to-do anything. Then, after a few weeks, if they get the urge to start a garden or build a shed or learn how to throw pottery, they have the time and the energy to do it. This no-planning approach works best with shorter leaves of a couple of months at most. Many people would be itching to get back to the chaos of the office after an extended period of doing nothing, and for some the desire to return comes even sooner.

A lack of planning can work if you plan to travel—that is, up to a point. Certain destinations, however, require advance reservations and deposits, and there are all sorts of restrictions on many foreign airline tickets.

Before you decide to not plan your sabbatical, take a close look at how you'd function without a schedule and think about that burst of adrenaline that accompanies every meeting where you just barely make it in the door before your manager glares at you. Take a weekend and don't plan a thing from Friday evening through Sunday night. If you have only an occasional awareness that there's something missing, you'll do fine. Better yet, take a week of vacation as a trial run and don't plan anything. See how well you do. If you're chomping at the bit after several days of doing nothing, you'd be better off setting goals and having concrete projects to work on during your sabbatical.

But if you luxuriate in being able to read a book, then take a nap, and decide what to do next after you wake up, you should give the no-planning method a try.

THE SABBATICAL FILE

Rosella Sabatini was working as an analyst at Goldman, Sachs in New York City in the spring of 1988 when she applied to and was accepted at the Yale Business School for the following fall. That same spring, a friend had asked her if she was interested in backpacking throughout Asia. Sabatini, an inveterate traveler, said yes. She quit her job in March and agreed to meet her friend, who had left earlier to visit relatives in Hong Kong.

The two women were not big on planning. In fact, all Anna, the friend, had told Sabatini was that she'd get a post-card letting her know when Anna would call so they could arrange to meet. Then Sabatini could tell Anna the date and time of her arrival at the airport so Anna could meet her. When Anna called, they spoke for a minute on the phone, and Sabatini prepared to leave. Previously, the women had not planned on exactly where they would travel, when they would leave, and for how long they'd be gone, figuring they would do all that later.

Even though their entire trip turned out to be spur of the moment, there were times when Sabatini wished it was a little more structured, even in the beginning. "Everything was set, I knew when my plane was arriving in Hong Kong to meet Anna, and I was on the plane the first time I panicked. I was supposed to look for Anna at the airport, and she's Chinese," she said. After a few moments of terror about what she would do if Anna didn't show up, her friend found her.

The two women spent the first few days of their trip in Hong Kong planning their itinerary. The only commitment they made was to buy one-way airplane tickets, called a circle flight, which had to be used within two months. "We also wanted to visit three or four specific countries, but beyond that, that was it."

Sabatini said that overall the lack of structure was occasionally harrowing, but it also turned out to be a lot of fun. They wanted to focus primarily on taking local transportation whenever they could, which turned out to be a mixed bag. "There were times when I was sick of carrying the backpack and being piled onto the trains like cattle, but other times I'd be amused by it. It wasn't a relaxing vacation, since we were doing a lot of overland travel. For one trip, we traveled to the rim of an active volcano, then we traveled on four different modes of transportation in one day: a ferry, a train, a donkey-drawn cart, then we rode on the back of some kid's motorcycle. Sometimes we didn't think we could take anymore," she said.

But the lack of structure was also the one part of her sabbatical that Sabatini enjoyed the most. "We got up in the morning and thought, 'Should we stay here, or move on?' We had enough flexibility in our itinerary so we could do that. We didn't put pressure on ourselves that we had to hit every single monument or cultural institution, although we did do a good job of learning about the culture. We spent a lot of time hanging out, meeting people, eating all kinds of food, and reading."

Over the course of the trip, the spontaneous traveling gave Sabatini a confidence she had previously lacked. "I came back from the trip feeling that I had more courage than I gave myself credit for," she said. "It gave me a balance and a new sense of perspective. I was really ready to do this kind of trip, and since Anna had already decided to do it, it made it easier for me to go. Even if I hadn't been accepted at Yale, I think I would have gone anyway. Now, I'm much more open to planning other kinds of adventurous trips, and I also try to bunch up my vacations so I can take it all at once and maybe do something like this again."

Whether you plan your time off down to the smallest detail, or decide to just plan the amount of time you're going to take off and figure out what you're going to do once you get there, be sure you know *why* you're taking off and how you expect to benefit from it. No matter what you decide, it's likely that you'll have to spend at least some time planning how you're going to be able to afford the time off. As you'll see in the following chapter, it probably won't be as hard as it seems.

5

Paying for Your Time Off

You'll need to have the money to support yourself and your family while on sabbatical as well as money to spend on what you want to do while you're not working. Although it's next to impossible to plan for a sabbatical without taking your finances into account, it's usually not the lack of money that prevents most people from taking a break from work. Indeed, the fear of what it will be like to lose the structure of how they spend a good chunk of their breathing hours is what stops most people dead in their tracks. Most people don't want to admit to this, so they use finances as an excuse to not even begin to dream about how taking a break from work would enhance their lives.

"Most people allow finances to serve as their major stumbling block when it comes down to deciding whether or not to take time off," says Nella Barkley, co-founder of the Crystal-Barkley Corporation. "But once we sit down and strategize exactly how they can do it, they are usually able to find a way to do it without getting overextended."

Many people use a combination of savings and, if it's allowed, cash in their vacation and sick time to finance their leave. Others have taken out loans or a second mortgage to pay for their sabbaticals and family leaves, or else they've rented their houses or a few rooms to cover their expenses. Although a few companies do provide paid sabbaticals to some of their employees, unpaid leaves are much more common. Probably the most that you can expect from your company is for your benefits to continue while you're gone. If you've mapped out the reasons why you want to take time off from your job, and have begun to plan what you're going to do on your sabbatical, then you're ready to tackle the financial part, which will probably be easier than you think.

After all, the things you choose to do on your sabbatical can also involve paid work in one form or another. It may not be the kind of work that you're used to doing, but it can be enough to pay some of your expenses and perhaps give you enough background so you can forge ahead into another career at the end of it.

"I don't advise my clients about finances," says leave consultant Neil Bull. "What is there to advise? Somebody knows what they have. They'll come in and tell me they've got four thousand dollars and four months, and I'll find something for them to do that will help them pay their expenses at home and away." Bull mentions a 30-year-old man he recently worked with who spent eight years in the aerospace industry. "He woke up one morning and knew he didn't want to spend one more day at his job," says Bull. The man came to Bull with $7,000 in savings and the desire to have a seven-year sabbatical. Everything that he does has to provide him with room and board; Bull says that's the easy part. So far, the man has worked on a ranch in Texas, on a farm in Ireland, and with the Iditarod Race champion Susan Butcher in Alaska.

"What he's trying to do is have enough experience so he can see what he really wants to do," says Bull. "He can always get a job."

Obviously, a single person with no dependents has an

easier time getting her financial house in order for a sabbatical. In many cases, though, families who have taken sabbaticals together have found it to be no harder to accomplish. In fact, even though it's difficult to arrange room and board for an entire family, especially when it is on the road, the amount of money a family spends over the course of a year on living expenses is frequently less than what they would have spent had they stayed at home.

Nine Ways to Finance Your Sabbatical

1. Sell or rent your home.
2. Get a foundation grant.
3. Max out your credit cards.
4. Cash in a life insurance policy.
5. Take out a home equity loan.
6. Fly around the world for free as an air courier.
7. Work two jobs for a few months before you leave.
8. Ask your boss to pay you three years worth of salary over four years, and take the fourth year off.
9. Exchange your annual bonus for time off.

Work Double Time Before You Go

Some people who take a sabbatical or family leave have to plan more carefully because they have no savings built up. They tend to take shorter leaves that don't require a lot of money for expenses beyond ordinary living costs.

Alisa Wechsler is an artist in New York City who supports herself by managing a retail shop in Greenwich Village. Her job normally consists of four ten-hour days, which leaves her with three full days a week to work on her art in her home studio.

Despite this chunk of time, she never felt that she ever had enough time to fully concentrate on her art. She wanted to have the opportunity to disappear for a month and do nothing but paint and sculpt all day. In early 1993, she applied for a month's residency at Yaddo, an artist's colony in upstate New York. A few months later, she found out that she was accepted for the month of June.

Although Yaddo accepts donations from its residents—artists and writers who come to stay for a month or longer—the colony also pays room and board and a small stipend. Even so, Wechsler had to be able to pay her rent and other bills in the city for the month she would be away and during which she wouldn't be earning her manager's salary. She also had to pay for the supplies and art materials she would use during the month, which tend to be expensive. To meet her expenses, Wechsler had to work extra days at the store. During the month before she left for Yaddo, and for the month after she came back, she worked one or two extra days a week, which covered about half her expenses for the month that she was gone. She asked her boss for the month off and the extra days of work about a month before she left. Since the summer is traditionally a slow time in her field, the other employees at the store appreciated picking up her extra hours while she was gone.

Another way that many people finance all or part of their sabbatical is by increasing their work hours before they go away, or by taking a temporary part-time job in addition to their regular job. Some even work double time after they return, although this can be a real shock to the system.

It's not for everyone, but working more hours before you leave will definitely make you appreciate the time you have all to yourself during your leave.

Men and women who choose to work extra hours can go

about earning additional money in a variety of ways: They can take a part-time sales job during evenings and weekends, help a friend who runs a business during a busy season, take on some freelance assignments in their field, or even do some odd jobs around the neighborhood, from running errands to baby-sitting. Temporary help agencies, however, aren't much help, because most only offer secretarial and administrative assistant jobs that take place during regular working hours.

If you plan to start a business where you're making a craft or some other tangible object to sell, it's easy to get a head start on your sabbatical. If you start your cottage industry six months before you're scheduled to start your sabbatical, it's possible that you could make enough money from it to live on during your time off. Once you're on your leave, you could make enough money to establish the business to the point where you're so successful after working on it during your leave that you don't have to return to work.

Earn As You Go

Cindy Mason considers the time she worked as a bicycle guide for a touring company to be her sabbatical. Starting in the fall of 1990, she took two months off from her job as a manager at a photo agency. She combined vacation time and unpaid leave and spent September and October leading bike tours in France and Italy. She returned to work, but when the biking company asked her to work again the following fall, she quit her job at the agency. "When I told my father I was leaving my job in the middle of a recession, he told me it was absolutely the stupidest thing he'd ever heard of," she said.

The job did pay her and provide her with room and board, but, as Cindy puts it, "We're not paid an extraordinary amount." Most bike tour companies in the United States pay their guides from $50 to $60 a day. For the first two years, she financed her time off by setting aside money during the months she was working at the photo agency. The rest of the time, she sublet her apartment to help pay the rent and to have someone there to watch over her cat. She also worked full-time on trips from March through November.

The reduced income did not scare her off initially. Instead, it was the expectations that she, her parents, and her peers had for the income she should be earning and the work she should be doing at this stage of her life that unnerved her. At 38, she was at least ten years older than most of the other guides she traveled with, and before she became a bike tour leader, Mason thought she was locked into her income bracket and position.

"I had a lot of stereotypical expectations of how much money I should be making and what I should be doing professionally, which was not what I wanted to be doing," she said. "It's really hard to separate the shoulds from the wants, since we all grow up with a lot of shoulds, and we all compare our incomes and positions to others to a certain extent." With all of these things swirling around in her mind, Mason at first found it very difficult to ask herself what really made her happy. But after she took the plunge and became a tour guide, she learned that she could live much differently on less money than she thought she could, while she worked at a job that was very different from what she had been educated to do.

Mason had always viewed her guiding job as a working holiday of sorts and said that she worked harder leading tours than she had ever worked at an office job. "It was far more complex on many different levels than I had expected," she said. "I was basically hosting a nine-day event in a foreign country for people who wanted a fabulous experience—they just happened to be on bikes. It surprised me how much of myself I had to give up and how little personal time and space I had."

While she was leading the bike tours, she didn't have a clear picture of where this job was taking her, whether she would continue to work for the company or switch to a new field altogether. "I got a lot of career counseling from my clients on the trips," she said. "I had been offered quite a few jobs along the way, and a group of lawyers had me convinced that I should go to law school. I just took it all in and stored it away for the future. I knew that I wanted to be happy in whatever I was doing, and in the meantime, I just loved leading the trips."

Now Mason works for an international travel company, a job she got as a result of her experience on the road. She's also making more money than when she was working at the photo agency. She still plans to take another sabbatical at some point in the future. "Once you get the bug in you, you're already thinking about the next time you're going to take time off," she says. "Right now, I'm ready to go rent a house in Tuscany. I can see taking a considerable amount of time off to pursue my photography. But now, no matter what I want to do, I know I can do it."

Running on Empty

Esther and Ben Burns of Chicago have virtually made a career out of taking time off from their jobs. Although they're retired now, they've taken 32 major trips over their prime working years; many of the trips involved taking time off from their jobs or quitting them altogether. They financed their trips in a variety of ways, although none of the trips were very well thought out in advance. Most often, the Burnses winged it, starting out with a chunk of money and returning home only when it ran out, which frequently took a year or more.

They took their first trip together a year after they got married and before their first child was born. "Ben had lost his job, and we decided to take off," says Esther. "I had a few qualms when he first suggested that we leave our jobs. I didn't know what we were going to do when we got back and didn't have a penny left. But somehow we always managed, although looking back, I don't know how we did it; we didn't have that much money to begin with."

The fact that they rented out their house and their longer trips were to third world countries made for inexpensive travel; their biggest expense was usually for gasoline. "Many of our friends and colleagues were dubious about us going to all these crazy places, but they were also envious and could have afforded it much more easily than we were able to," says Esther. "But it was a matter of choice, and what we wanted to spend our money on. We wanted to see the world. Other people needed their security more."

Sometimes, Ben, who worked as an editor and writer, wrote freelance articles about their trips, but they didn't pay much and didn't begin to pay their bills. Saving a bit of money in advance, along with renting their house while they were away, would usually be enough to cover their travel expenses.

When they got back, Esther—who taught school and was able to receive a number of unpaid sabbaticals from her jobs over the years—would usually be able to find work right away. "The thing that stops most people from taking time off is worrying about the security they'll have coming back," says Ben. "Our philosophy was that things would always work out when we got back. We had enough confidence in our ability to function, so we had a sense of security that we would find something. Neither of us has high demands when it comes to luxuries; we spend our money on travel, not on material things. Sometimes I did get a little queasy about having nothing to come back to, but the experience of travel and meeting new people is more important to us than new furniture."

Budgeting for Your Sabbatical

No matter what your financial situation is, it's important to draw up a budget that you'll follow during your sabbatical. And if you don't already live on a budget, it's a good idea to draw up one now so you'll have an idea of where you need to spend your money and where you can cut back. It also helps to have a present budget, so that you can have something to compare to your sabbatical budget.

The following scenario of one woman who went on sabbatical shows how she played with her finances to arrive at a budget that would be comfortable for her.

Jean Cooper is an account executive at an ad agency in a suburb of a major city. One of her accounts switched to another agency in June, and she knew things would be slow over the summer. So she combined a month of vacation time with two weeks of sick and personal days and two weeks of unpaid leave to take all of July and August off so that she could stay at home and paint landscapes.

A friend who also painted had taken what she referred to as an extended vacation the summer before to spend a month painting at her parents' summer house. Her friend came back so energized that Jean immediately started making plans for her own sabbatical for the following summer. Even if her account hadn't left the agency, she would have still found a way to go.

Jean had fixed expenses she had to take care of, but some of the expenses in her budget would be eliminated because she wouldn't be working. Unfortunately, these savings were eaten up by her need to buy art supplies and take one private lesson in addition to a group class during each week of her sabbatical. These extra expenses turned out to amount to more than the money she would save, so she used some cash from her savings account to cover her expenses for the two weeks of unpaid leave. She also cut out extras like a couple of dinners out a week, unnecessary makeup, and all the two- and three-dollar items she buys on impulse each week.

Here's Jean's regular budget followed by her sabbatical budget:

Regular Budget (for two months)

Income
$600/week take-home pay
Total: $4,800
Fixed Monthly Expenses
Housing: $700 rent
Utilities (gas, electric, phone): $70
Food: $200
Car expenses (insurance, gas): $150
Credit cards: $200
Car payment: $300
Entertainment: $200
Savings: $200
Miscellaneous: $90
New clothes: $150
Lunches out: $140
Total: $2,400

Sabbatical Budget (for two months)

Income
Four weeks paid vacation: $2,400
Two weeks sick and personal time: $1,200
Savings account withdrawal: $1,200
Total: $4,800

Fixed Monthly Expenses
Housing: $700 rent
Utilities (gas, electric, phone): $70
Food: $200
Car expenses (insurance, gas): $150
Credit cards: $200
Car payment: $300
Entertainment: $200
Savings: $200
Miscellaneous: $90
Art supplies: $100
Lessons: $160
Total: $2,370

During her sabbatical, Jean was able to save $290 a month because she didn't have to buy new clothes or lunches. Even though this savings was eaten up by her art lessons and supplies, she still came out $30 ahead. If she wanted to take a few extra lessons or buy more materials, she could go out less often and put only $100 into her savings account for each of the two months she was off.

Here's your own work sheet. Figure out your fixed expenses and areas where you'll save money and where you'll need to spend extra. Also look for ways to offset an imbalance, like cutting back on nonessentials or pulling some money out of savings.

Regular Budget (for X months)

Income
$_____ take home pay
Fixed Monthly Expenses
Housing (rent or mortgage payment): $_____
Utilities (gas, electric, phone, cable TV): $_____
Food: $_____

Car expenses (insurance, gas): $_____
Credit cards: $_____
Car payment: $_____
Entertainment: $_____
Savings: $_____
Miscellaneous: $_____
New clothes: $_____
Lunches out: $_____
Total: $_____

Sabbatical Budget (for X months)

Income
Paid vacation: $_____
Sick and personal time: $_____
Savings account withdrawal: $_____
Total: $_____

Fixed Monthly Expenses
Housing (rent or mortgage payment): $_____
Utilities (gas, electric, phone, cable TV): $_____
Food: $_____
Car expenses (insurance, gas): $_____
Credit cards: $_____
Car payment: $_____
Entertainment: $_____
Savings: $_____
Miscellaneous: $_____
Additional costs: $_____
Total: $_____

By analyzing the above totals, you'll be able to determine:

☐ How much money, if any, you'll make in salary during your leave;

- ☐ How much savings you'll need to withdraw;
- ☐ What expenses you will be able to eliminate; and
- ☐ What you will need to spend extra money on.

Should You Go into Debt?

Although many men and women who go on sabbatical use a combination of savings and pared-down living expenses to finance their leaves, some do not hesitate to go into debt. Those people who have a guaranteed job upon their return are most likely to go into debt, because they know they'll definitely have the income to pay it back once their leave is over.

Still, even though countless Americans have taken out loans for special trips and vacations, it makes some people queasy to think about borrowing money in order to finance an extended leave—perhaps because it seems so selfish to take time off for yourself.

One advantage of taking on debt to finance your sabbatical, of course, is that you can eliminate your money worries during your time off, which will allow you to better focus on what you want to accomplish. The main disadvantage is that you have to pay the money back. If you borrow money to finance your sabbatical, at least try to arrange it so that the first payment isn't due until after you return to work. Otherwise, the pressure of having yet another expense when you're trying to cut back can be enough to distract you from your main purpose for taking a sabbatical: taking a break from the rat race.

Here are some questions to ask yourself before you borrow money to finance a sabbatical. Write your answers in your notebook. If you're considering going into debt so you'll have enough money for your sabbatical or family leave, it's a good idea to ask yourself the following questions *before* you fill out the loan application:

- [ ] What's the least amount of money you think you'll need to borrow? Can you cut it down even more?

- [ ] How much time will you need to pay it back? What if you decide halfway through your leave that you don't want to return to your job? How will the loan be repaid?

- [ ] How do you plan to borrow the money—by personal loan, a second mortgage or home equity loan, credit cards, your credit union, or from a friend or relative?

- [ ] Can you delay the first payment until after your sabbatical ends?

- [ ] What if you come back and find that you're out of a job, even if it was guaranteed?

Of course, if it doesn't bother you to go into debt, go right ahead. But sabbaticals have a funny way of changing the way people think and react to their previous lives after the sabbaticals are over. And then some people just decide they have to take time off no matter what, so they take on however much debt they need.

Steve Seigal was working at IBM in Boulder as a development manager when he applied for and was accepted for a one-year paternity leave starting in July of 1986. The company didn't have a formal paternity leave policy at the time, so he took the leave under the company's Personal Leave of Absence program.

He was the first man in the history of IBM to take a paternity leave, and the country didn't ignore this fact. Seigal made it into *USA Today*, *Cosmopolitan*, and *Sesame Street Magazine*, and other national news media. Several other men at the company took paternity leaves shortly afterwards. IBM gave Seigal two weeks of paid time with the rest unpaid; and full benefits continued throughout the year. His wife, Alice, a veterinarian with her own practice, took five months off after their daughter was born before she returned to work. The only preparation that Seigal made before the leave involved his finances. "It was very hard to predict what kind of system I was going to use with my wife to make it all work, so I concentrated on deciding what we would do to support ourselves while we weren't working." Before he went on leave, Seigal took out a second mortgage on his house as a line of equity credit that he could draw from as he needed to pay for living expenses. He viewed it as a replacement for his salary.

He paid it back in the first eighteen months after returning to work.

Three years later, when their first child was four years old and a second child was eighteen months, Seigal applied for and received a second leave of absence in order to spend more time with his family. He financed this leave the same way. Seigal had always done some work at his wife's practice, but he tended to squeeze it in after his responsibilities at IBM were through for the day. Partway through his second leave, Seigal began to think about not returning to the company. While he was gone, IBM developed its early retirement package for certain employees, and the day that his leave was up, Seigal resigned from IBM and began to work full time at the clinic.

THE SABBATICAL FILE

In 1976, Noel Aderer, who today lives in Marlborough, New Hampshire, was teaching special education at a Connecticut high school when she decided to spend her summer vacation traveling west with her dog. As the trip progressed, she realized that the last thing she wanted to do was return to the classroom in the fall. She reluctantly returned, but applied for a leave of absence for the following year, which she received. Aderer says that her last year of teaching was made easier by the fact that she knew she wouldn't have to do it again.

During her year off, she planned to spend her time working at a few different jobs, relaxing, and traveling throughout New England. "I started off knowing I wanted to do something else," she said. "I didn't plan anything, everything was sort of serendipity."

She owned a small house and cottage in Connecticut that she rented out, which provided her with an income that financed her year off. She also worked at a couple of jobs for a while in southwestern New Hampshire. When she was in Connecticut between trips and/or jobs, she lived with her parents, who had a house in the same area.

"Everyone thinks that owning a house ties you down, but renting it was the one thing that enabled me to take time off," she said. "And I knew if things didn't work out, at least I had a house and a job to come back to, which gave me a lot of confidence. I could put myself at risk for a year and feel I could risk going out to find something else."

Aderer had grown up riding horses, but all the time she was living in Connecticut, she found that it was too expensive to ride; in addition, she didn't have the time. Once she was on her sabbatical and exploring northern New England, however, she began to think about riding again.

Although she hadn't ridden for 12 years, one thing led to another, and she bought a horse that spring and boarded it at a neighbor's sheep farm. A few years later, Aderer started her own farm and began raising horses and renting out a few bed-and-breakfast rooms, again allowing her real estate to finance what she says has turned into one big sabbatical.

"Now I only do the things I love to do," she says. "If I enjoyed today and enjoyed yesterday, and look forward to tomorrow, that's more than most people in the whole world have."

"When I was working at the school, the money was good and my pension was accruing, but I kept hearing about people who retire and get injured or sick, and never enjoy their time off because it comes so late. Suddenly, the idea of working your whole life to retire didn't make sense to me. I felt that my life should be what I'm living for and not my retirement. When I first announced that I was going on sabbatical, everyone told me that they thought I was so lucky, but first I had to totally stop caring about money. If you start to work at something you love, the money eventually comes," she said.

Handling Your Finances While You're Away

If you're traveling out of the country, or even within the country, but you plan to be out of touch for long stretches, you'll need a trustworthy friend or relative to deal with your finances, pay bills, depositing checks, and balance your financial statements.

If you're traveling domestically, you'll be able to write the checks yourself, although it's difficult to get mail forwarded if you're not going to stay in one place. Better to make a clean break from your everyday life and feel like somebody else is paying the bills for once.

Depending upon how long you're going to be away and how many bills you expect to pay over that period of time, the best way to handle your finances is to sign several books of checks and have a good friend fill in the amounts and send the bills out before their due dates. This person should also pick up your mail at least once a week, so give her your post office box key or alert the post office or delivery person and neighbors that someone will be picking up your mail. It's a good idea to arrange to call this person once a week, preferably on the day she picks up your mail, so you can deal with any emergencies right away.

You should also talk to your banker and arrange to have payments for your mortgage and other loans automatically deducted from your checking or savings account. Usually, all you'll need to do is write a letter authorizing the bank to do this for the amount of time that you specify.

If you're going to be out of the country during the first third of the year, arrange to have your W2 statements and other verifications of your income automatically sent to your accountant. Bundle up as many receipts and deduction statements as you can and drop them off at your accountant's so that he can prepare your tax return and send it in by April 15. Or, you can choose to do an estimated return, although you still have to pay the taxes in advance.

Money on the Road

Once you've scrupulously scrimped, saved, and budgeted for your sabbatical, you don't want it to be difficult to access your money while on the road. Several of the people I interviewed for this book took their traveling sabbaticals before the wide availability of ATM machines. They had to rely primarily on bank transfers, wires, and travelers' checks. All three are still viable options today, but there are easier ways that are both cheaper and more expensive.

Today, especially if you stay in the country, withdrawing money from your banking accounts with an ATM card is the easiest way to carry money for your trip. However, you may find you stray from your budget because it is so convenient. Also the access fees can add up. You might pay $2 or more for each transaction at a machine that's on your network but is not your bank.

Overseas, you can use ATMs as well, although they tend

to be located in the larger towns and cities. Ask at your bank to make sure its ATM is hooked into the major international networks like CIRRUS or Plus.

Another way to get money on the road is by activating a cash advance from your credit card, although this is really borrowing money. It's also a good idea to renew your cards before you leave if they're due to expire while you're away. Make sure that all monthly payments are made so that your cards are not canceled.

You can also have money wired to you or arrange for bank transfers, but these options have their drawbacks. In a remote location, it can be difficult to locate an affiliate of Western Union or other wire service, and with bank transfers, it can take two weeks or more to receive your cash, because the money has to pass through so many different banks: from your local bank to an international bank like Citibank or Barclays, to a large bank in the country where you're located, and finally to the branch near you.

A combination of travelers' checks, ATM access to your checking and savings accounts, and judicious use of credit cards usually works best.

How to Get Somebody Else to Pay for It

Whether you're planning to do something splashy, take up an activity that will benefit people (like a volunteer position), or to pursue a craft (like create enough work over the course of your sabbatical so you can mount an art show in a local gallery), it might be possible to convince a company or two to pick up the tab.

That's what Jordan Schaffel did when he convinced Nikon, Fuji Film, DHL, and Pan Am to chip in on the cost of his 12-month round-the-world trip.

First, he believed in his project and goals, even when his

parents and friends didn't. When one company turned him down, he went to the next one on his list.

Next, he gave his project a twist. Anybody can travel around the world taking pictures. Schaffel's sales pitch to Nikon, however, was to promote international culture and show different people in different countries using a camera for the first time in their lives. Once he got Nikon's approval, he approached the other companies. With Nikon's approval, Schaffel was able to easily convince the other companies to finance a part of his trip.

He also promised the companies something in return for their generosity: unique pictures they could use in their own promotional materials. The cost to the companies, was, actually, minimal. Some companies have a finite budget for donating equipment and services, while others agree to a certain number of projects that catch their eye. In any case, each of the companies that sponsored Schaffel received photos that they otherwise would have had to pay tens of thousands of dollars to get from professional photographers.

Many people are surprised to learn that most large corporations have a department designed to do nothing else but give its products away, for matters other than just free advertising. As it turns out, these corporate gifts are a write-off for companies, because they most often consider such gifts to be part of their promotional and marketing budget. Because most departments receive thousands of requests for free equipment and services annually, you have to have a unique project to catch their attention. You'll improve your chances of gaining a corporate sponsorship in one form or another if you follow these guidelines:

- ☐ There has to be something benevolent in nature about your project.
- ☐ Your sabbatical has to make the sponsoring company look good.

☐ The company has to believe it's getting something tangible in return.

If you're determined to get corporate sponsorship, look at your project through the eyes of the person or committee that will be evaluating it. If one company turns you down, keep going until you find one that will accept your project.

Oh, and don't forget about approaching your own company. Your success and their apparent goodwill in granting you a leave in order to go off and do all this important stuff will sound wonderful in a press release.

Legal Concerns

More than one sabbatical has been cut short when a pressing business or financial matter at home has come up and there's no one around who can deal with it. That's why some people, especially business owners and people who rent out their homes, should appoint a friend or associate to serve as power of attorney should an important legal issue need to be addressed while you're gone. Sometimes, an important legal decision has to be made in your absence, such as a tax matter or a problem that might come up with the tenants who are renting your house. For example, if you wish, the person whom you appoint power of attorney can determine that your tenants are in violation of their lease and begin eviction proceedings against them.

Another legal issue that might concern you involves child custody. For instance, if you share custody of a son or daughter, will your ex-spouse agree to it if you want to take your child with you on sabbatical or out of the country? Or, if you're planning to be away for a few months without a visitation even though your divorce decree specifically states that you must see your child on a certain number of days per month, do you think that your ex will use your violation of the agreement to push for full custody? Before you leave, whether or not you take your child with you, sit down with your lawyer to discuss all the possible problems that could arise with your custody arrangements should you choose to be out of touch for a while.

How to Spend Less Money on Your Sabbatical Than If You Stay at Home

If you're like most people, you'll probably have to spend some time building up your savings so that you can afford to take the time off. Most of that money is going to go for basic living expenses like rent, food, and utilities. Many people who travel have to stick to a strict budget, which is often less than what they'd ordinarily spend if they remained at home working.

This is especially true for families who travel together and who plan to do a fair amount of camping out. Children will presumably be away from the insidious influence of TV commercials and the pressure of their peers to have the latest of everything. The emphasis will be on companionship, and while eating out in restaurants can get expensive, many families will find that this will get old after a while. Coolers can stock a couple days worth of food from the supermarket, so the major expense turns out being gas.

How Much of a Monetary Risk Are You Willing to Take?

When you quit your job in order to take some time off, there's always the chance that when you do find work after your

(Continued)

(Continued)

break, you'll have to get used to a drastically lower salary, at least for a while. In your notebook, ask yourself the following questions before you quit your job to take a sabbatical, especially if you're going to use it to test out a new business or career.

☐ How much money have you budgeted to live on both during and after your sabbatical?

☐ Do you think of yourself as a risk taker?

☐ If you had suddenly to get used to living at a level one-third to one-half of what you're used to, could you do it if it meant you were working for yourself?

☐ With your loss of salary comes a loss of status. Do you see it as a threat if you don't have a job with which you and others can identify with?

☐ What will your immediate family think? Will your decision to accept a lower salary put a crimp in any of their plans, like college or an addition to the house?

How to Take a Sabbatical If You're Broke

Sometimes it's an ironic truth that the less you have the freer you are. People who have fewer ties to a job usually have less money and, therefore, also know how to make do with less. It's usually easier for them to take a break than it is for someone holding down a $100,000-a-year job and dealing with all the ties and debts that usually accompany that lifestyle.

It will also be more in keeping with your character if your income is modest. People won't be as likely to think that you're nuts if you decide to step off the merry-go-round, because you probably aren't a card-carrying member of the Corporate Ladder Climbing Club of America.

So, if you're flat broke and want to take time off, here's what to do:

1. Find a job—any job—that will allow you to pay your basic expenses while you sock a hundred or more dollars away each week. Work for three to five months or until you save enough on which to live.

2. Cut your living expenses to the bone. If you can live with someone in exchange for the housework and cooking, do it.

3. If you're like me—and as a freelance writer and pianist, I'm always finding myself in the near-broke or broke category—when you finally do have enough money, you're probably going to want to hit the road for your time off. Make sure your wheels are functional and that you're prepared to face several months of cheap eats. Come to think of it, again, if you're like me, you probably don't have to do much preparation for this aspect. Then, just go.

4. Your sabbatical will probably be the spontaneous type. (See "How Not to Plan, chapter 4, page 72). You'll probably have to do even less planning than is specified in that section.

5. Do you belong to any clubs or associations with a nationwide network of members? I've known people who have traveled around the country solely staying in other members' homes for a night or two. I'm a member of the American Society of Journalists and Authors, with almost 900 members nationwide as of this writing. Although some members do offer rooms to members for a fee under a special bed-and-breakfast program, I know that many of them will let a traveling member crash for a couple of nights, especially those in remote areas. The better to compare notes and gossip.

6. If you're broke and want to take a sabbatical, but don't want to have to work for a few months in order to save up enough money, consider selling a big ticket item or several

smaller ones in order to finance your sabbatical. For some people, it's not enough to move out of their homes or quit their jobs. Every so often, there are a few who need a break so badly that they'll sell everything to finance it: the house, the car, the furniture, and the clothes, with only enough left over to fill not even half of an average-sized rented storage unit. It's not an easy thing to do, getting rid of most of your possessions, but for some people it's just the ticket, and it completes the picture of totally disengaging themselves from their previous lives.

Other Ways to Get Extra Money

The following advice is only for a hardy few, but if you ever really want to get away from it all, consider one or all of the following:

☐ Sell all of your worldly possessions, except those you can fit in the biggest piece of luggage you're taking along with you, whether it's a backpack or the trunk of your car. If you don't need the money that badly and don't want to take such drastic measures, then put some of your things in storage.

☐ Similarly, make a list of the things you absolutely need to take. Then get rid of everything else.

☐ Put your house on the market a year before you leave. If it sells, you may have a big enough chunk of cash to allow you to take several years off. If it doesn't sell, contact a property management company and arrange it so they'll handle all the headaches of renting your house.

☐ Sell your car, especially if you're still making payments on it. You can buy another cheaper one if you're planning to stay somewhere else. Or, if you're traveling extensively, do it all without a car and see how much your life really slows down.

☐ Leave your dog, cat, and assorted other pets with a friend or relative so you won't have to pay money boarding them. (Your pet will also be much happier.)

THE SABBATICAL FILE

In the mid 1980s Kathy and Rob Merrill were living in central Massachusetts, working too hard, and hating every minute of it. Rob had graduated from medical school in 1984 and finished his residency in 1987 before he went to work for a local clinic. Kathy had been working for AT&T as a statistician since 1982. Before Rob started his residency, the couple began talking about taking some time off a few years down the road. After Rob completed his residency, they began planning their sabbatical in earnest.

"When I saw Kathy come home every day after commuting 90 miles, she was absolutely beat," says Rob. "Even though we had a great income, there was a lot in our lives that was really lacking, and none of it was fun. We didn't realize how much we were postponing in life, and we learned that living without is the way for us to live."

They knew they would travel on their sabbatical, and they had fantasized about going to every continent in the world, traveling with only the packs on their backs. "It was a good time to do it before we decided what we wanted to do with the rest of our lives," said Kathy. "We had been married for six years, with no children, and I was leveling off at my job. I was at the point where I was either going to change jobs or quit."

The Merrills narrowed down the list of countries they wanted to visit—Tahiti, Australia, Nepal, and France among them—and then set a target date of May 1989, for their departure. They deliberately left the end of the trip open, because they weren't sure when or if they were going to come back. "If we fell in love with Nepal and wanted to do missionary work, then we wanted to be able to do it with no problems," said Kathy.

Once the date was set, the Merrills got busy. They sold their house, cars, clothes, and household items, and gave their cats to Kathy's mother. The rest of their belongings they put into storage. They totally cleaned house because they wanted to raise money for the trip, and because they wanted to let go of their previous constricted lives. This turned out to be an important part of their sabbatical. "It was quite a freeing catharsis, because once we felt we could take that first step and get out of the rut that we thought we were trapped in, we realized that nothing is forever," said Kathy. "I saw that if I had to, I could change my life that drastically again."

"Before we left, we talked to a lot of people who said we were crazy," said Rob. "They couldn't believe we could just walk away from everything. More than a few friends said, 'Think of all the money you could have made while you were away.' And for years, I felt trapped in that same rut: Should we buy a new car this year? Which Caribbean island should we go to for vacation?" Rob says that, for a while, it was pretty easy to get caught up in the idea that these were things that he and Kathy needed. "But," he says, "we had to work a lot of hours for those things. And in the end, what it really came down to was how much money we weren't spending because we didn't have a mortgage or car payments." In fact, the couple lived on no more than $2,000 a month during their travels.

Money wasn't an issue for the Merrills, but they did meet a lot of people traveling around the world who were literally living on a dollar a day. "We knew that we didn't want to get to a country and not be able to do anything," said Rob. So they alternated between camping out and staying in hotels, and since they had a good cushion of money—for third world countries, at least—they didn't have to worry about not being able to afford it.

They ended their trip nine months later in February of 1990 when they became burnt out on traveling. "Being a tourist gets old after a while," said Kathy. "Besides, we started to think about what we were going to do when we got back." They also came down with giardiasis, an intestinal illness that's spread by drinking contaminated water, and they were sick for almost two months.

Once they returned to the United States, they stayed at a friend's apartment and tried to figure out what they wanted to do next. "We immediately felt unemployed once we got back," said Kathy. "It was amazing, but within days of returning, I started to feel very insecure about not having a job," said Rob. "I started sending out resumes, and I even got some part-time work at my old clinic. But we didn't have a house anymore, or a car, and we were still living out of our backpacks. It was a real letdown."

Rob looked for jobs at medical offices and clinics in central Massachusetts and southern New Hampshire, but after their trip, they found they didn't want to live in a densely populated area anymore. "I was overwhelmed by how many people there were in Asia, that when we came back and found the same thing in Massachusetts, I immediately wanted to leave again," said Kathy.

Two months after they returned, the Merrills decided to move to Maine. Rob began his own private practice in family medicine, which is something he thinks he wouldn't have done if he and Kathy hadn't traveled around the world for the better part of a year. "It gave me a sense that we could adapt to new challenges and make decisions on the fly," he said. "I went into private practice on a bank loan and a handshake, and I don't think I would have done that if we hadn't traveled." Instead, he says he would have taken the safe route and joined a group practice with a guaranteed income and a lot of commitment in a metropolitan area.

The Merrills also don't feel the need to travel anymore. Before their sabbatical, they went skiing out west and frequently went away on weekends. "I think we dropped the pretense that we have to always be doing something fascinating," said Rob. "In a strange way, I feel like I'm still on a trip. It's easy to get back into the materialistic groove, but for a short time we were able to enjoy living out of our packs."

6

Negotiating with Your Boss

The difficulty of going to your boss and asking for a break that constitutes more than an extended vacation from your job may make the planning and financial end of a sabbatical look easy. But even the most hard-nosed boss may say yes to your request to temporarily leave your job and keep your benefits and status intact.

Some employers are naturally more amenable to approving time off for their workers than others, and obviously, the more valuable you are to your company, the more likely your boss will be to work with you to give you what you want. Creative businesses, industries that normally employ a large stable of freelance help, and businesses for which a surfeit of workers usually exists tend to be among the more sabbatical-friendly fields. Industries like law and communications, where employees work on a project-by-project basis, make it easy for an employee to take off between projects, and then come back to dive right into the next one.

In order to convince your boss to give you time off, it's necessary to present your leave from the standpoint that it will benefit both you and the company. Therefore, you have to do your homework and take a very proactive stance right from the start.

There is still a lot of resistance from managers who think that time away from work can only be negative to the business, so it's important to stress the benefits your leave will have on the workplace, both during your sabbatical and after you return.

Some informal studies have shown that leaves cut down on employee attrition; the rest and relaxation of a sabbatical or family leave means that the worker will come back refreshed—and grateful. A company with a sabbatical program will find itself with a workforce of very dedicated employees. After all, if the company is going to offer every worker an extended amount of time off on a regular basis, employees will think they should work that much harder when they come back. Frequently, if an employee is at the point where time off is necessary to their health and sanity, and the company won't grant a break, the worker may just quit. "Companies have to realize that the notion of stepping out is not a failure or threat to them," says Neil Bull. "It's very positive, since they're recharging people. In some companies, people who aren't able to convince their bosses of the need for time off will just walk away. The businesses that realize this will be able to hold on to these people for the long haul."

Of course, it doesn't hurt if you're invaluable to the company. You stand the best chance of getting your company to agree to your sabbatical if you're an employee at mid-management and up who has given the company five or more years of service. It also helps if you've regularly pitched in beyond what was expected of you and are someone who other workers regularly turn to for advice on business and personal matters.

Of course, your boss may say that you're too valuable to let go, even for a short time, but you can always counter this by asking what it would be like at the office if you decided to leave permanently.

First Things First

The first thing you should do is mention to your immediate supervisor that you've been thinking about putting in for a family leave or sabbatical. Don't make a big deal out of it; just mention it casually, allow him a brief reaction, and then say something like, "I've worked it all out, and I'll drop off the details later in the week." Then change the subject. Your boss might react with, "You must be kidding," or "Great, I'll be looking for it." The important thing at this stage is not to let his initial reaction kill your enthusiasm.

A few days later, drop off your proposal, and stick around while your boss reads it. Then be prepared for any questions. Try not to get defensive if you are told it's impossible. Instead, stay calm and reinforce your convictions by stressing how your leave will benefit the company. If the answer is still no, try again in a few weeks, and let your boss know that you're serious.

It's not a good idea to go over the head of your immediate supervisor. This can create big problems down the road if his supervisor says yes to your request after your boss has said no. Offer to compromise on the time you need off, or offer some other sweeteners that will convince him to say yes. Either way, one of two things will happen: You'll either wear him down after a while, when he sees that you're not going to give up, or he'll use some other excuse to eventually fire or demote you so that you're not in his face anymore. Although you may not want this, at least you'll have your sabbatical, and you can go looking for another job.

As Nella Barkley says, "You've got to approach your boss first with the advantages your leave will have for both the manager and the company. And unless you're able to outline them, you're not likely to get it."

One advantage, according to Barkley, is that you will return. In fact, companies with formal sabbatical policies on the books often penalize workers who don't return or who leave within six months of returning from a leave. At McDonald's, which rewards full-time employees with eight weeks of paid leave after ten years of service, if an employee quits a job within six months of returning after a sabbatical, that worker must pay back to the company the salary he received during the leave.

Another advantage is that time away from work will help the employee to view work from a different perspective upon her return, and to recommit herself to the company.

If the company doesn't need to hire a replacement during your leave, the economic advantages to the company are the primary benefit. But with a paid sabbatical, the benefits tend to be more esoteric than economic. The price of improved morale at a company that provides every employee with a paid leave is impossible to count in dollars and cents. One woman who worked at Lotus, a company that provides every employee with a month off with pay after five years of service, says she dedicated herself to the company even more after she came back from her leave. She describes another company that she worked for in the past as anti-employee. "Nobody ever did anything extra for the company," she said. "We were lined up at the door at 5 P.M."

Drawing Up a Sabbatical Proposal for Your Boss

Five major points to be covered in a proposal for a sabbatical of any length are:

1. What you're going to do while you're away.

2. Why you want to take the time off.

3. How long you need to be away.

4. How your responsibilities at the office will be covered in your absence.

5. How your sabbatical will benefit the company.

The total proposal can be a page or two, long enough so that each point is succinctly covered. However, you need to do as much advance research as you can so that you can answer any unforeseen questions that may pop up.

For instance, there's the perennial favorite: "What if you don't come back?" For some bosses, no amount of reassurance will convince them that you love your job enough to return. "Why, then, do you want to leave it?" will be the response.

It might help ease your boss's fears if you also tell him about the projects you plan to start working on when you return to your job and also mention that your increased energy and enthusiasm will do wonders for your efficiency and, therefore, help the company. Of course, if you have even the slightest inkling that you don't plan to return, you probably shouldn't mention it.

Here, then, is the proposal a CPA submitted to the firm where she worked for seven years. Note that she scheduled her leave after April 15th and before June 10th, after tax season but before work on quarterly taxes begins at the firm.

To: Leonard Mulligan

These are the details for my six-week break that we discussed last week. I would like to request a six-week leave from work for the period from April 20th through June 1st so that I can take a much-needed break after tax season and also from the events of the past year, when I was promoted to department manager. I plan to use a combination of my standard three weeks of vacation, one week of personal days, and two weeks of unpaid leave to accomplish this.

This break coincides with my nanny leaving and my need to find another. It will also allow me to spend a significant amount of time with my three-year-old son Josh.

The company will benefit from my leave because I will return well rested and better able to focus on the two new significant projects scheduled to begin this summer. I will also be more content when I return to work because finally, I will have been able to see what it's like to be a regular mother for a while. Probably after a month and a half of being at home, I will be very eager to return to the office.

This time of year is ideal both for me and the firm. Since half the staff in my department plan to stagger their own vacations over this period, my supervisory skills are not needed in the office. My associate Lynn Tucker will be available during the entire period to assume my responsibilities if necessary.

The company does not need to hire a replacement for me, thus saving $1,400 in my salary alone, due to my two weeks of unpaid leave.

I have given the company seven years of loyal service, and hope that the company sees that by granting my wish for a leave, my loyalty will be engendered even more.

Respectfully,

Joanne Frost

Playing Your Cards

Staying Connected

Taking time off from work doesn't necessarily mean that you have to cut yourself off totally from the office, although many people choose to do just that. The flextime and job-sharing programs instituted in many companies in the 1980s provided a way for employees—particularly parents—to scale down at work while still keeping a hand in what was going on at the office. The same might work for you and be just the thing that puts your boss over the edge to say yes to your request for time off.

Negotiating to do part of your work during your time off, or at least touch base with the office once in a while, will help keep you in the sight and mind of your colleagues and soothe your boss's fears that you might not return. You can do this even if you're traveling. "With technology the way it is today, you can work at home or at foreign locations and keep in touch while you're away," says Nella Barkley.

Elizabeth Suneby chose to stay in close contact with her company, Work/Family Directions, in Boston, during her maternity leave. When she joined the company in November 1992 as the vice president in charge of marketing, she was four months pregnant, which the company was aware of when she was hired. A little over half of her leave was paid; she left in the beginning of April 1993 for 14 weeks of maternity leave.

Although the company didn't require it of her, Suneby wanted to keep in touch with her colleagues during her break, and at one point she even interviewed several job candidates at her home. "As the head of a department, and also since I was relatively new, I wanted to be on top of certain things," she said. Suneby had a fax at home and chose to work on certain projects, keeping the option for the right of first refusal, where she would pass on projects if she felt too overwhelmed.

Before she went on leave, she identified the major projects that were underway or were scheduled to begin while she was gone, and she specified the staff member who would head up each project, with another employee who would act as support. "Everyone warned me against committing myself to all that I thought I could do, and because this was my first baby, I didn't know what to expect," she said. "My coworkers left phone mail and faxes for me, and I had the option of picking them up or not."

Work/Family Directions is a very employee-friendly company; it made *Working Mother* magazine's Top 100 Companies to Work For annual list. Her superiors gave Suneby the option of staying involved or bailing out when she wanted, and she definitely appreciated the flexibility. In the first three months of her leave, she wanted to stay connected to what was going on in the office. But when the end of her leave was nearing, she decided to totally disconnect from her department and announced a self-imposed two-week blackout period.

"The core belief at the company is that you have to help people balance work and family to get the most out of your employees," she says. "I work very intensely and am just as serious about my career after I became a mother, but I have a much better perspective and will probably do even a better job because I have more diversity in my life." Before she left Suneby worked hard to get her department in order, both in terms of handling the workload and assigning responsibilities in her absence. "Do what you can beforehand to feel good about leaving things at work," she says. "It's important for the company, for yourself, and if you're a manager, for the people who work for you."

Building Your Case

As with the other aspects of planning for your sabbatical, doing your homework in advance doesn't hurt. Being able

(Continued)

(Continued)

to convince your boss that your leave will benefit the company is no exception. Answer the following questions in your notebook, and here, especially, try to anticipate every move that your boss will make so that you can prepare your own defense.

☐ How do you think your boss will react to your request for a leave? How can you prepare in advance for your meeting?

☐ How willing are you to negotiate for time? If you want three months off and he offers only six weeks, would you be able to restructure your sabbatical?

☐ How can you present your leave as a benefit to the company? How will your absence negatively affect the business? What can you do to temper this?

☐ Will it be necessary to hire a replacement? Will the boss be more amenable to your request if you agree to keep in touch once a week?

☐ What sweeteners can you guarantee the company after your return, i.e., any new knowledge that will help to increase productivity, you'll stay on at the company for at least two years, and so forth?

☐ Secretly, do you think there's a chance that you won't want to return to the company at the end of your leave? If so, what and when will you tell your boss?

Cutting Loose

When you're already working for a progressive company, you don't have to have hard facts to convince your boss that you need to take a break. But when you're approaching an old-school boss who sees your request for time off as disloyalty at best and a thinly veiled desire to quit at worst, your rationale has to be totally different. Even if you never completely win your company over, although you do get your leave, you have to do your best to convince the powers that be that it was the right move. You might, however, spend the rest of your days at the company doing so.

In this case it's probably better to totally disengage yourself from the company during your sabbatical, especially if leave taking is rare. Dropping by every so often to say hello and catch up on the latest can easily make your colleagues resent you—whether or not you're their boss—and this resentment can last long after you return. You have to weigh what would be best, and usually this can be determined by the reaction to the announcement of your sabbatical. If your co-workers think that you're getting special privileges that aren't available to them, a complete break might be best. If, however, they greet your news with happiness and undisguised, good-natured envy, then they'll probably look forward to having you touch base every so often. But you might want to steer clear of your boss during your visit.

For one of his sabbaticals, Ben Burns gave up a partnership at a Chicago public relations firm when his wife Esther took a leave from her teaching job. They left in July 1968. When they returned in May of 1969, he went back to the agency as an employee.

Although none of his employers ever held a job open for Burns, they all expected him to come back after the leave was over. "He'd always do a lot of the work beforehand," says Esther. "His bosses didn't like it, but they put up with it. I have a very adventurous husband, and he's also very well organized."

But even on the first day that he returned to work, Ben was already thinking about the next trip. "I always hated PR," he said. "For me, it was just a way of making a living. I always went back, but it was just a routine I had to go through until the next trip."

How to Make Your Boss Say Yes

If you have a tiger for a boss, it might be easier to save enough money for your sabbatical than to get him to agree to let you take a leave. With some bosses, getting them to agree even to a compromise could be considered a major victory. If your boss is in the habit of compromising, perhaps you should start out by asking for twice as much time as you really need. That way, if he offers you half the time that you asked for, well, that's the kind of upper-hand guy he is. And you are right where you want to be.

Whether you're trying to convince your mother that you're doing the right thing or to win over a colleague at the office, it's possible to employ a few techniques designed to at least bring them down a few notches. You may never be able to convince your most ardent detractors of all the good reasons for taking a sabbatical, but, then, who knows? With your strong debating skills and a successful sabbatical of your own, you might find yourself helping them plan their own time off at some point down the road.

The first thing to do when you set out to steer any argument your way is to try to convince your opponents that your idea is their idea. In other words, try to figure out how *they* will benefit most from time off, and then make their reasons your reasons. Get them thinking about why they'd want to take a break.

What would they enjoy most about a sabbatical? Would they like the time off to relax or to pursue a hobby full-time? For instance, if your boss loves to tinker with his car, what would it be like for him if he could just wake up in the morning, head out to the garage, and spend all day at it, instead of having to come into the office? Let your boss know you're willing to play the guinea pig. Then when you come back from your sabbatical, you can help him plan his.

Covering at the Office

Your boss will be much more likely to agree to let you go if you tell her that it will be almost as if no one notices you're gone; the office will run that smoothly without you. This also will endear you to your co-workers, who may fear that they'll get the brunt of your work added to their already heavy workloads, and at no extra pay.

The first thing to do is to strive for a naturally slow time at the office, because if you don't need to hire a replacement, in essence you'll be saving your company money. Also, doing some of the work ahead of time—like planning or starting new projects by spending an extra hour or two on them at the office each day before you go—may pave the way.

If you have a secretary or administrative assistant, show her how to deal with potential problems in your absence. She'll probably appreciate the extra responsibilities and the faith you place in her. In addition, it's a good idea to ask for her input for future projects that she can do while you're gone.

Of course, you have to convince your manager that your assistant will be able to handle anything that will come up while you're gone. If necessary, assuage the company's concerns by arranging to call in once a week or so to follow your assistant's progress and answer any questions that may have come up. Only if it's necessary, leave a number where you can be reached in case of an emergency or only during specified hours. You want a sabbatical from your job; you don't want to be sucked back in by a boss or assistant who wants to sabotage your leave.

If it's not possible to leave during a slow time at the office, reassign certain projects to other employees for the duration of your leave. This doesn't always work, of course, especially if you need to transfer some work to a co-worker with whom you don't get along. In this case, use your instincts and assign this person a project that you believe he would really enjoy and make his own. It will help if he's not already overburdened with work and if it's a project that's usually handled by someone above his level. Flattery and trust in his abilities may go a long way towards patching the rift between you. Then, when you come back from leave, offer the project to him on a permanent basis, pending the approval of your superiors and assuming he did a good job.

How do you handle reassigning your projects to a fellow employee whose workloads might already be stretched to the limits? Bribery always works well. A couple of well-placed business lunches or dinners, a hint that she'll be the first to know about future positions at the company that you know she'll be interested in, or the promise of a glowing letter of recommendation for her next career switch will go a long way. Then again, if you're the boss, what you say goes, and you can do whatever you want.

If, however, you know in advance that a co-worker is going to resent doing your work when you're off—which means that there's a good chance that it won't get done or that it'll get done wrong—then don't even bother to approach her.

Reassigning your workload is a touchy subject, so use your instincts to decide what would be best for you and your colleagues.

Will You Need a Replacement at Work?

Of course, sometimes you'll have no say in whether your boss decides to hire a replacement for you in your absence. It does, however, serve as a bargaining chip in the negotiation process if you can convince him that a replacement is unnecessary and thus save the company a lot of money.

A lot depends on your level and your job. If you're a secretary or administrative assistant, there are legions of skilled temps out there who can replace you in a minute—actually, maybe too easily. But if you're a supervisor or the head of a department, replacing you will be a little trickier. In this case, more often than not, extra work will be spread around to your colleagues. How will they feel about that?

In the end, it's all up to your company. Employees in similar positions with the same number of staff and responsibilities at different companies—or even in different departments within the same company—will undoubtedly find that they get a variety of responses because one boss thinks it's a fine idea, while another thinks it's the dumbest thing he's ever heard.

If your boss belongs in the latter category, do your homework first and make sure he has as little ammunition to use against you as possible. If you think that not hiring a replacement will help your cause for time off, then answer the following questions in your notebook:

- ☐ If you're taking your leave during a slow time at the office, what will still need to be done while you're gone? Is it possible to do it ahead of time? Could your assistant or a colleague pitch in when necessary?

- ☐ How much of your work can you feasibly do in advance? Could any of it wait until you return?

- ☐ If your boss still thinks you need a replacement, will a part-time temporary worker suffice?

- ☐ What does your company do when you go on vacation? Is it possible to take their typical solution to dealing with your absence and multiply it according to how long you need to be away?

If You Definitely Need a Replacement

If you and your boss decide you do need a replacement, you'll have to find someone who can take on your role, do it for a short period of time, and then step down. Your boss probably won't want to take on the extra work of locating such a person.

Look at the role you play at your job. Then come up with a plan to have that role covered for as long as you're away. Says Sandra Bunnell, who left her job at an advertising agency to take her second sabbatical: "I wanted to find my replacement, train that person, and get everything in order so I could leave, and have a smoothly running procedure to enable me to do that," she said.

"It's very unusual for a company to think in this way, but it's a very orderly way to institute a transition."

Making Up the Time

One novel way to take time off from work is to build up a surplus of hours by working extra hours both before and after your leave. This way your salary continues while you're gone. This is the equivalent of working extra hours to earn extra money, assuming you're paid by the hour. Storing up hours on salary means you still get paid while you're gone, and you get a chunk of time off.

Say you'd like a month off from work, and you already have two weeks of vacation coming. If your workweek is normally 40 hours and you work 50 hours for each of the eight weeks preceding your leave, then you will have worked two extra weeks in two months; this period can be added to your two weeks of vacation. Or you can break it up and work extra hours before and after your leave, although it might be difficult to go from a sabbatical straight back into a 50-hour week.

The idea is to get creative so that your leave works out for all involved: you, the company, and your co-workers. This is just one way to work it so that everyone comes out ahead. See what else you can come up with.

THE SABBATICAL FILE

Elliot Hoffman started to plan for his sabbatical five years to the day before he took off. "In 1988, I told my family and key people at the bakery that in five years, I would take a year off and also change my role at the bakery when I returned," said Hoffman, owner and co-founder of San Francisco's Just Desserts bakery.

Each year that passed during his countdown, Hoffman would announce how many years were left until he would take his sabbatical. "I kept reminding everybody to let them know that it was very real to me. That old cliche kept coming up: At 95 and on your deathbed, how many people say they wished they'd spent more time at the office? I wanted to spend more time with my family," he said. In 1993, when he began his sabbatical, Hoffman's son had just turned thirteen, and his daughter was seven.

He had a lot of negotiating to do at the bakery, and his planning was painstakingly detailed. He worked with a steering committee and a group of close friends who are consultants, and together they developed a plan whereby Hoffman would bring on a general manager to assume his responsibilities. Eighteen months before his target date, Hoffman and his board began planning how they would hire his replacement. A year in advance, he informed his key management staff of 30 about his plans. The manager would come on board at least eight months before Hoffman left for his sabbatical so the two could spend a good deal of time together. "My year off would be a break for me, but also time for the new general manager to build a relationship with the staff without having me constantly looking over her shoulder," he said. "It was also time for a change in the day-to-day leadership for the business, and someone with new skills and energy was very appropriate."

For the first few months his sabbatical progressed as he

had planned traveling with his family. However, once he returned home, real life intervened. He was called into the bakery to help straighten out some problems and ended up getting sucked right back in, which scared him, since he had planned his time off for so long. Hoffman recognized what was happening, and he managed to extricate himself again from the business before too much time had elapsed.

"I never thought I would totally unplug from the company when I left on my sabbatical," he said. "I thought I would meet with the general manager on a monthly basis, and with the steering committee every quarter." Hoffman resumed this schedule after his initial crisis. He also found that his employees generally approved of his desire to take time off. "Everyone was very supportive," he said. "I think they liked the fact that someone in my position was taking a different view of life."

When the Boss Wants a Break

Sometimes the boss, too, wants a break, and he has to negotiate with the employees, or at least his top management staff. When Ben Strohecker decided he wanted to take a year-long sabbatical from Harbor Sweets, the luxury candy company he had founded, he announced his plans 18 months before his target date and made sure that all of the responsibilities of his management group were set in place. He arranged to have his executive vice president/chief operating officer replace him, and the two of them planned to meet quarterly during his sabbatical to go over the numbers and discuss the business. He started to phase out six months before he left.

Unfortunately, as the year progressed, Strohecker and his replacement discovered that there were some things that were falling through the cracks. The problem was that Strohecker didn't want to usurp his replacement's authority, but at the same time she was overly apprehensive about taking too much responsibility away from him. He admits that the two of them should have had more contact during the year he was away, but he says that this turned out to be the only weak link in the entire transition.

Going back to the business was a mixed bag. "It was one of the best years we ever had in the business," he admits somewhat ruefully. "But I was determined not to demote anybody when I came back, and yet, I needed a job." As a result, when he returned, he says that he had the feeling that he wasn't pulling his weight, and he and his COO were walking on eggshells for several months before everything got back to normal.

Pat Newlin, who owns her own public relations agency in New York, also had to work out a plan with her employees when she left the company for two months in the spring of 1993 to live in Paris and write a novel. Like Strohecker she kept in touch with her company, and though she didn't have to negotiate with a manager to take the time off, she did take her employees into account.

"I figured that two months would be a legitimate amount of time that I could be away without making myself crazy about what was going on with the company," she says. She hired an interim president to run the company, and she met with every employee to iron out any expected kinks before she left. She also installed a fax machine in her Paris apartment and promised her employees that she would be in the apartment for an hour every afternoon Monday through Friday, so they could contact her with problems.

When she was sitting in the cab that would take her to the airport, she looked up at her office to see her employees waving good-bye at her, and she panicked. "I thought, 'What am I doing? I like these people, I have my own company, it's all working, and now I'm leaving,'" she recalls.

She needn't have worried. She finished her novel and returned to work two months later, already planning her next sabbatical. She said she would have taken time off sooner if she knew how great it would turn out for her. She also returned to the office encouraging her employees to take time off. Even before she left on her sabbatical, Newlin had developed a company leave policy where, instead of taking a raise, an employee could take the amount of money of the raise and convert it into additional vacation time.

What's Good for the Goose Isn't Necessarily So for the Gander

When Elliot Hoffman returned to work from his sabbatical, he thought about instituting a formal sabbatical policy at Just Desserts, but he wasn't sure how realistic it would be. "When we started the business, we worked without a day off for three years," he says. "I make no apologies and feel very comfortable telling people that I deserve this time off, I want this, and I'm going to do this. That doesn't mean that everybody else in the company can do this. No one else created this business." As it is, every employee at the bakery already gets about a month off from work through vacation days, personal days, and holidays. "If I were to pay for five or six weeks of vacation, would my customers be willing to pay a few bucks extra for a chocolate cake?" he asks. "I don't know."

This attitude is typical for many business owners, according to Neil Bull, who works with what he call "hotshots" of the Young Presidents Organization—members who are presidents of their companies before they're forty. Bull says that these guys think the idea of a sabbatical is wonderful, but not for the people in their companies. "They think, 'Let somebody go?' These guys are super-A types anyway, working 94 hours a week, and they can't fathom it because they never had a sabbatical. The people down below think that it's great, but if the CEO doesn't think so, it's not going to go," he said.

Hitting a Brick Wall

What do you do if you've planned out your sabbatical, drawn up a proposal for your boss, pointed out the money she'll save and the new-and-improved employee you'll be upon your return, and she still says no? There are still some options to try.

Borrowed Time

In 1988 Susan Cox, a reference librarian at Dartmouth College in Hanover, New Hampshire, wanted to take a day or two off once a week or so to care for a friend who was terminally ill. However, she had already used up her vacation and personal days for that year, which amounted to about a month.

Cox went to the human resources staff member at the library, said she had to have the time off, and asked about her options. She specifically asked about the possibility of borrowing some vacation and personal days from the calendar year 1989. Cox had been at the library for ten years when she made her request, and it was granted.

She ended up borrowing almost all of her vacation and personal time for 1989, which meant she had to borrow vacation time from 1990 and beyond in order to have a vacation each year. By 1993, she had barely caught up.

Combined Time

If you lump all of your vacation, sick time, and personal days together, would the result be enough time for you? Would your boss agree to grant you a week or two of unpaid leave to bolster your time?

Even in companies that offer paid sabbaticals, employees frequently tack on vacation time or other guaranteed days off, or even add on time without pay. This can frequently add up to a substantial amount of time off, sometimes up to two months or more.

Slow Time

Wait until the company experiences an economic downturn, and ask again. There's a lot more flexibility for allowing time off when money is tight and employers are looking for ways to cut their costs. As a result, they tend to be more approachable; whereas in good times, your leave—even an unpaid leave—could very well affect profits, in terms of lost productivity.

One Step at a Time

It might also be possible to leave your job gradually, cutting back a day or two a week at first, then staying out for a solid month or two, before gradually easing your way back in, a couple of days a week at a time.

Their Loss, Your Gain

Just quit.

7

The Naysayers

No matter what you say about taking time off, some people—
your friends, your family, your co-workers, anyone else who
happens to overhear your plan—are going to think you're
crazy. Either that, or they'll be absolutely green with envy
when you tell them that you've decided to take a year off
from the grind.

Many are called, but few choose to take time off. Deciding to take the plunge and quit work, either temporarily or
permanently, takes guts and commitment. Once you decide
that this is what you're going to do, every person in your
circle will have a definite opinion; a neutral stance is rare.
Often a negative response will come from a person who
doesn't think he could ever do what you are doing; he probably thinks that he doesn't have what it takes to operate
without the safety net of a full-time job.

Sometimes the naysayers will try to discourage you because they think you're either shirking your responsibilities
or deserting your family, or because they don't like the project
you are undertaking. Well, you're going to plan and go on
your sabbatical anyway, but it would make everything easier

if your primary support network was on your side from the start.

Take your notebook and write down your answers to the following questions:

- ☐ Are you allowing your family and friends to stand in the way of your sabbatical?
- ☐ Can you think of anything to help convince your family and/or friends that you're doing the right thing?
- ☐ What can you do if, despite your best intentions, the people around you are being negative about your plans to take time off, and are trying to talk you out of it?

Some Drop by the Wayside

Ben Strohecker, who took a year off from his company to work on AIDS issues, says that some of his friends and acquaintances didn't understand what he was trying to accomplish. "People who were casual friends are still asking me if I'm on my year off. The people who know me well and who realize that I've always worked in community service were very supportive of what I was doing."

Because he was working on AIDS issues, some people became very uncomfortable around him. "It separated my real friends from the casual friends," he says. "The acquaintances were very uncomfortable with it. They wouldn't even mention the word AIDS around me, and I could tell that they were afraid that I might. They didn't quite walk on the other side of the street, but it was a good personality test. The people who could handle it turned out to be better friends in the end."

The Top Nine Reactions to Your Sabbatical and How to Respond to Them

Whenever you tell someone—a relative, co-worker, or stranger—that you're planning to drop out of the real world for a while and, for a change, do what you want to do, you'll probably get one of the following reactions. Feel free to use any of the responses included here. (If you get a response that's not on the list, write and tell me so I can add it.)

1. "Are you nuts?"

   Response: "Yeah, ain't it great!" Send postcards and bring back lots of souvenirs and stories. Never mention the troubles you encountered.

2. "Why are you throwing your job/life/future all away?"

   Response: "I'm just putting it on hold for a while."

3. "That's what *I'd* like to do if I could have a sabbatical."

   Response: "You can." Encourage him to do what you're doing. Show him your sabbatical plan and the proposal you gave to your boss.

4. "But why does your boss want you to take six months off?"

   Response (even if it's not true): "Because I'm a wonderful employee, and she wants to reward me."

5. "Aren't you scared?"

   Response: "Of course. But I want this so badly that I'm pushing the fear onto the back burner."

6. "How wonderful!"

   Response: "Thank you, I know."

7. "How can I do it, too?"

Response: "Here's what I did." Keep him updated on your progress during your sabbatical, and help him to map out a plan once you return.

8. "Can I come, too?"

Response: "Where and when do you want to go?"

9. "Why are you going when I can't?"

Response: "What makes you think you can't?"

Winning Over Naysayers

☐ Involve them in your project. Give them periodic progress reports to let them know what a terrific time you're having, or bring them souvenirs from your sabbatical.

☐ Help them out if you can. If you're staying at home, you're probably going to have some extra time—at least more than you'd have if you were working full-time. What would help melt their resentment? Baby-sitting? Bringing them to a class or workshop so they can see how you spend each day?

☐ Offer to help them plan for their own sabbatical. If they refuse or say it's impossible, do it anyway and then give them the plan. More likely than not, they'll be flattered instead of angry, and it may help to defuse the tension between you.

☐ Be mysterious. Drop clues every so often, especially to resentful co-workers. For instance, send them an anonymous note with some object you produced on sabbatical that mails well. Publicists do this to win over editors and producers. Why not you?

THE SABBATICAL FILE

Once you've decided to take a break from work, you'll see many advantages to doing so. Don't, however, assume that your managers and colleagues at work will agree with you. Dan Morris, who took off six months in 1993 to travel, said that the board at the food co-op where he had worked as a manager gave him mixed reactions when he handed in his letter of resignation.

"There were a few people who were very upset that I was leaving the store only six months after we had moved and expanded it," he said. "It was such a huge project that they felt I wasn't following through. Other people reacted with anger, which totally surprised me. They said, 'Why are you doing this to us?' They didn't think anything about how I was feeling in the wake of the move, and so I had to sit down with each one of them to tell them about why I needed a change."

Morris adds that even without the negative reactions of certain board members and some of the other employees, he worried about their response. "Part of me thought that I was letting down the membership and staff if I did what I wanted to do, and also about what people would think in general about me if I left," he said.

His friends thought his decision to take time off was great; they supported him fully and told him they thought he should have done it sooner. "They saw a real change in me in the first few months. I was more laid-back and was spending more time with my friends, most of whom I hadn't seen in a while." But a few members of his family, especially the older ones, didn't understand. They asked, "Why are you doing this when you're on the corporate ladder? Why are you going down when you should be going up?" His grandfather, however, who died while Morris was on sabbatical, thought it was great. "He told me, 'Do what you want to do, and do it now,'" said Morris.

Although he had quit as manager of the co-op, the board told him he could come back to work in a full-time capacity in a lower staff position at the end of his leave; technically his sabbatical was a temporary leave of absence. When he returned in September of 1993, he once again faced very mixed reactions from the board of directors and the new management team that had replaced him. "They were very nervous about having me come back in a nonmanagement position, because they were concerned that the old staff would still treat me as a manager," he said. As a solution he decided to work two part-time jobs—one at the old co-op and one at another co-op—instead of one full-time job so that he could specifically avoid going too far in the direction he was heading before he took his sabbatical. "Before I left, I wondered about who I would become at the end of my sabbatical, and if I would be able to achieve the goals I was hoping for," he said. "What's happened is that I'm holding on to the feeling that I had during my time off, and working part-time helps me keep it, although some of my colleagues and friends still don't understand."

Recently he was offered a third part-time job and decided not to take it, because it would have meant going against everything he had worked for during the six months of his sabbatical. "It was a really big step for me to say no and not overextend myself," he said. Now Morris works four days and plays the other three. "A manager's salary could never pay me to do what I'm doing now," he says.

Family Resistance

Morris seems to be living the type of life that many people dream of, but the pressure from friends and family can be such that you never are able to voice your ideas about taking a sabbatical. You may keep the plans under wraps until the last minute, which is especially hard when you're planning to bring the whole family with you, and you're a public figure to boot.

"My 16-year-old son thought it was the most embarrassing thing he'd ever heard of, a six-month vacation," said Lamar Alexander. Most everyone else he'd been in contact with, however, understood the *why* perfectly. They just didn't understand the *how*. "Everyone I know has dreamed about it at some point in his life, I mean, dropping everything, packing two bags, taking the family, and moving halfway around the world where nobody knows you," he said. "I think that appeals to mostly everyone. Then everyone asks 'How?' Americans are afraid to leave their jobs; mostly they're afraid that they'll lose out and get behind and they'll get bored by doing nothing. They're so used to doing something, which is precisely why someone like that should do this."

He says that since his return, he's become a sort of ambassador of sabbaticals and he'll talk about his experience with anyone who'll listen. He even wrote a book, *Six Months Off*, about his experience.

Although his son originally balked at the idea, he and the other kids admit that they wouldn't have traded the sabbatical for anything. "Usually with a family, you each go about your lives and rush around passing each other like planets," says Alexander. "But when you're 16 and 13 and don't know anyone else in town and you're just sitting and staring at each other, you might as well talk. For six months, we really had no one else to talk to except each other, and at times, it could be a very harrowing experience. On the one hand, we're a much closer family and a great deal more dependent on each other, but at the same time, each member of the family is much more independent." Although Alexander had planned specific jaunts to destinations that he wanted his family to see, he intentionally kept their time off relatively unstructured. He suggests that other families who are considering taking time off together plan to make it a happy and fun experience, and lean towards making it easy rather than hard.

What If Your Kids Don't Want to Go?

Admittedly, if you were one of those kids who grew up with the cheery exhortation, "This is a family vacation and you're going to have a good time whether you want to or not," you probably are a bit sensitive about the issue of whether to force a kid to do something as radical as leave her friends for six months against her will.

But since, in retrospect, you also are able to see the good that eventually came of it, you're feeling a bit torn. Should you make a reluctant child leave all that's familiar to accompany the family on sabbatical?

One way to deal with this dilemma is to take the kids before they're old enough to have a voice in the matter. Indeed, several of the families I interviewed said that the impetus for the family sabbatical was the fact that at least one child was on the verge of adolescence.

However, even if you do encounter opposition, you still have several options. One is to insist that she come with you. Another is to let your child stay behind, living at a friend or relative's house while the rest of you go off on your wonderful adventure, and let her know every step of the way what she's missing.

But if you sense she, too, would like to go away—just not with her family—perhaps you could suggest that she look into becoming a foreign exchange student for the time that you're gone.

Regardless of which option you and she pick, it's almost guaranteed that if she stays home she will regret it.

What If the Naysayer Is a Spouse?

You're all excited about the plans you've made, but your partner is less than enthusiastic. What can you do?

This is a tough one. Especially if you plan to travel. One way to approach it is to take turns. Others will view it as a way to take a sabbatical from the relationship, which may, in fact, be necessary.

In any case, you should make it clear that this is something you have to do for yourself and that it bears no reflection on your relationship. However, it can be a way for you to examine both yourselves and your marriage, and then either make a new commitment to each other or decide to let go.

Kelly Madden of Columbia, Missouri, taught in Portugal for two years, and her husband went through a lot of soul-searching while she was gone. They regularly exchanged letters while Kelly was abroad, and she found that her entire perspective of marriage had changed in the interim.

"I thought that being married meant 'You do 50 percent, I'll do 50 percent,'" she told the magazine *Special Report*. "Now I think that if you really love someone, you don't think in terms of 'this is what I do and you have to meet this line.' My decision to go to Portugal triggered problems in my marriage, but it also accelerated solutions. We've both changed a whole bunch."

How to Stick to Your Guns in a Swelling Tide of Negativity

When there are very few people who support your decision to take a sabbatical, it can be hard to keep your spirits up, not to mention your motivation. You may even begin to lose interest in planning your sabbatical.

Here are some suggestions to help you overcome the anxiety that negative criticism from others can provoke:

- ☐ Don't let them affect you. Even if they do affect you, pretend they don't.

- ☐ Continue to plan. Use their negativity to inspire you to prove they were wrong.

- ☐ Regard yourself as a shining role model. Assume they're just jealous and want to see you fail, because they don't think that a sabbatical is a possibility for them.

- ☐ Try to win them over. With each negative statement they toss your way, tell them about the latest thing you've done to plan your time off.

- ☐ Ignore them. Pursue your dream even harder.

8

The Sabbatical

Okay, now you're free. What are you going to do, and how will you structure your days? It all looked good on paper, but unless you have a plane to catch, the fact that you don't have to get up and go anywhere will probably catch you off guard.

Setting Goals

The only way that many of us know that we're getting anywhere is if we set regular goals and then reach one before proceeding to the next. A sabbatical where your aim is to accomplish something concrete is no different.

The goals that you set depend on how you're spending your sabbatical or family leave. Some of these goals will be tangible; others will be intangible. For instance, say you want to spend three months traveling around the world. You set a goal of wanting to visit eight different countries during that time. This is a tangible goal, and it's probably the one that's foremost in your mind.

But say somewhere in the back of your mind you also

think that the travel will enable you to slow down your pace, drastically at first, and then continuing after you venture back into the real world. The goal of relaxation is an intangible goal that frequently is measured only when you look back and compare your new calmer self with the chaos-imbued presabbatical maniac that you once were.

Undoubtedly, you'll have your own specific goals—both tangible and intangible—that you're interested in accomplishing during your time off, but you can use the following checklist to help you set your goals before you begin your sabbatical. Keep in mind that not all will apply to you.

In your notebook write the answers to the following questions:

- ☐ How much of what you're doing do you want to accomplish? For instance, if you want to spend your time off writing short stories, how many do you want to have completed at the end of three months?

- ☐ If you're working in another business for six months to see if you're cut out for it, how will you know in the end that you are?

- ☐ How do you want your life to have changed by the time the sabbatical is over? It's important to set postsabbatical goals, at the same time that you decide what you want to accomplish during your time off. Although it's difficult at this point to envision what your life will be like after your sabbatical, let alone how you'll change in the meantime, it is still crucial to plan for how you're going to follow through.

- ☐ How do you want what you've gained during your sabbatical to carry over when you go back to the real world? In the case of the short story writer, will you set a goal of one new story every month, or one hour of writing a night? Or, if you spent your time off working with an antiques dealer, will you plan to open up your own antiques shop within a year of ending your sabbatical?

☐ How do you see yourself doing things differently once you return to work or after your sabbatical ends? What stopgaps can you put into place to remind you when you start to slip back into your old habits?

Tracking Your Progress

Again, in some cases, it may be pretty difficult to know in advance how quickly and in what way you will progress. But if you draw up a rough plan ahead of time and match yourself up against it every week or month of your sabbatical, you'll have a something to tinker with as you proceed.

Hint: If you're like me and tend to drastically underestimate the amount of time it will take you to accomplish a certain task, do yourself a favor and overestimate the length of a project. One of your aims during your sabbatical should be to find your natural rhythm of working. Frequently, the frenzied pace at which we are accustomed to handling piles of paper tends to obscure the depths we can reach in our work. And if you're the type who enjoys checking items off your priority list more than doing the actual tasks themselves, look to your sabbatical as a way to begin to enjoy working for its own sake, not as a way to earn a gold star on some amorphous chart.

If you're in this category of overachievers, it may actually be worth your while not to formally track your progress, and instead learn to luxuriate in the task itself with no thought of whether or not you're keeping up. This method is bound to make you uneasy at first. But I guarantee that if you learn how to work this way for a long enough period of time, and at the end can look back and marvel at the quality of the work you were able to produce, then at least if you return to the old way of doing things, you'll look upon it with a different eye.

Being Flexible

When I write a book, I draw up a proposal and table of contents, but I know that by the time I've written the last word, the content of the book will just barely resemble what was in that early outline.

As I've said before, it's important to use a sabbatical to discover the ways in which you work best. Think of those studies conducted to determine whether a person is a lark who works better during the day, or an owl who functions better at night. I've never known how owls are able to get anything done during lark time, and vice versa. When you first begin your sabbatical, you may well undergo what Ray Daniels referred to as a detox period, especially if you've held a high-stress job with lots of overtime. It may take you a while to catch up on your sleep, so if you need to take several naps a day in the beginning, then do it. But frequently, closing your eyes for a half hour is much more refreshing than a two-hour nap, after which you may awake feeling groggy and unable to work.

If you're concentrating on one project for your sabbatical, then experiment with a variety of work styles. Work in spurts, spending perhaps only an hour on one part of your project before you switch to something else, or do all of your work in one sitting until you're done. If you favor one type of work habit, try the opposite to see how you do. Your sabbatical, after all, is all about experimentation. Being flexible about how you work is only one way to do it.

You should also try to be flexible in switching between

the various smaller projects that make up your sabbatical. If you hate doing something, stick with it for a while, even if your natural inclination is to give it up. Along the same lines, if you would prefer to work on just one aspect of your project the entire time, even though there are nine other areas that you planned to explore, then resist the temptation to continue your focus and instead switch to something else. You may find that it's easy to return to where you left off, and that the momentum you've built up doing the thing you like best will carry over to the other parts of your project. It may even enable you to see certain aspects of it that you wouldn't otherwise have seen.

For example, say you want to develop a complete photographic portfolio by the end of your sabbatical. Your natural tendency might be to shoot all the pictures first, then develop them, and then mount them, because this efficiency was necessary when your photography was but a hobby that you fit into the few spare hours you had when you were working full-time. Instead, try playing around a little. Shoot a few rolls of film, then develop them, and then decide how to mount them. And then shoot some more, and start the whole process over again. It may be that this method results in greater quality and depth of work than did the old scattershot approach.

How to Work and Still Feel Like You're on Sabbatical

Of course, for some people, working in any other job but the one they've been programmed for is a sabbatical of sorts. However, even the novelty of a totally different job can wear off after a while, especially if it in any way resembles your regular job (even working the same number of hours and days).

(Continued)

(Continued)

Because this is your sabbatical, you should break out of your rut. Keep your sabbatical job fun and fresh.

☐ If you usually work days, arrange for your sabbatical job to take place at night, if at all possible. You'll have your days free, and you'll really be able to feel free when you see everybody else rushing off to work every morning while you're only on your second cup of coffee.

☐ Work only part time. If you're using your sabbatical job to decide whether to switch to another career, you can usually get a pretty accurate picture of that career working only 20–30 hours a week. This leaves the rest of your time free to explore other areas of interest.

☐ Perhaps the best way to disprove that your sabbatical job isn't really a job is to do something you wouldn't do at your regular job. So, if you need to take some time off from your sabbatical job, do it. Take a break for a few days, if you feel like it. Just make sure in advance that your new, temporary boss is aware that this might happen. After all, this is your time to spend as you wish.

Switching Gears

Too much planning can kill the joy of taking a sabbatical or family leave, just as too little can make it seem unproductive. Say you want to explore three different activities over the course of your year off. It's a good idea to initially plan to spend equivalent amounts of time at each pursuit. However, you should always build in enough flexibility so if one idea really catches your fancy, you'll be able to switch gears and concentrate on that one project. After all, taking time off is about the structure—or lack thereof—that you place on yourself and not what somebody else dictates to you. Even though you may work at a job that isn't considered high-stress and in a place known to be laid-back, you may still be a prime candidate for a sabbatical.

When Dan Morris planned his sabbatical, he knew he would spend part of his time traveling, so he scheduled two major trips: one to England, the other to Alaska, along with a number of other shorter trips throughout New England. He saved up his money, bought his airline tickets, and left his job in March of 1993. The first week, he left for England, where he spent three weeks. During April and May, he stayed at home, spending his time canoeing, hiking, biking, and taking day trips around Vermont and New Hampshire. In June he left for Alaska, and although he had originally planned to stay for six weeks or longer, he decided it wasn't what he wanted, and he came back after only three weeks. Then he visited Nantucket, which wasn't included in his original plans, before returning to work. Even though he had to change his itinerary in the middle of his sabbatical, Morris still says that his time off was perfect because he did what he wanted when he wanted.

Perhaps the secret to having a successful sabbatical is this flexibility, this ability to fine-tune as you go along and not stick to a rigid plan, even if you discover shortly after beginning that it's not what you expected. Are you the type of person who feels you have to finish a book when you've already read the first three chapters and think they're lousy? Likewise, you shouldn't think you have to stay in a particular place just because that's how you originally had it planned. A sabbatical is a once-in-a-lifetime experience—at least your first one is—and you shouldn't feel compelled to do anything you don't want to do. It's time to spoil yourself, and if it means leaving a country a few days or weeks early, then do it. This, of course, is one of the big advantages of traveling without an itinerary. If you don't have a particular schedule, it will be much easier on your conscience and pocket-book because you won't be losing money and undoing your plans, but you'll be getting what you want to get out of your sabbatical—the freedom to finally do what you want.

From the moment he started thinking about taking time off, Nick Leeming built flexibility into his year off from school. In the spring of his senior year of high school, he was burned out. Leeming was a student at a college prep school and for years had been on the fast track heading towards college and a corporate job. But he wasn't happy with the direction in which he was going, so his parents suggested that perhaps taking a year off before going to college would be a good idea.

"At first I thought, no way, because no one else in my class was doing it," he said. But it quickly began to grow on him because he was so burned out from working hard in school and applying to colleges at the same time. "I thought that a year off would recharge me, and that I'd get to travel. I wanted to get away from the academic setting, and have the chance to use a different part of my brain. I knew that this was the best time for me to do it, because I had no dependents and I wouldn't lose time off from a job."

He worked with Neil Bull of the Center for Interim Programs, who, after an intensive brainstorming session, drew up an itinerary for Leeming that included three months at the National Outdoor Leadership School in Wyoming, six weeks working at a dive shop in Micronesia, and three months in Italy working as a gardener. "I felt so free, it was the first time in my life that I was really independent," he said. "I got on a plane in Boston and flew halfway across the world to a place I'd never been to be with people I'd never met. It was incredible to do something that I really wanted to do, with no deadlines for papers."

Taking a Break

I alluded to this in chapter 4, but I'm mentioning here just to make sure you're prepared. It may sound strange, but the time might come that you need a sabbatical from your sabbatical. Either you've been working very intensely and need to reconnect with the family and friends you've been ignoring, or else you want a real vacation and need some perspective. Even if you're spending your entire sabbatical traveling, being on the road for a number of weeks or months can be extremely tiring, especially if you're staying in a different place every few nights or so.

If you need some time off from your sabbatical, think about the most decadent thing you could do: spend a week in a remote cottage by yourself, go to New York to spend the weekend window shopping, or take a week doing nothing more than being with your kids every waking moment. Chances are that you're going to be stressing your brain in ways it hasn't been stressed in years. Partway through your sabbatical, you might need to gain some perspective into why you've taken the time off in the first place. One of the best ways to do this is to go to the other extreme and choose a no-brainer for an activity. I'll bet after you finish your sabbatical from your sabbatical, you'll be itching to get back to your sabbatical.

Extending Your Sabbatical

Chances are that as you near the end of your sabbatical, you'll discover that you either need more time or aren't yet ready to face going back to work.

If you want to hold on to your job and your status in the

office, it's probably not a good idea to ask for an extension of your leave. Your boss may well offer you the option of a permanent leave. However, even if you do get an extra couple of weeks, the co-workers who kindly agreed to take on some of your work a few months ago probably aren't going to be crazy about having their increased workload continue for longer than they had thought.

If you're halfway through your leave and think you're going to run out of time before you achieve your goals, then this is probably a good point to evaluate what you've accomplished so far and take a look at what's left. Then you should chart out a plan for the remainder of your sabbatical where you can intensify your efforts so that you can accomplish everything you need to by the end.

But sometimes stepping up the pace will just make it that much harder to go back to work. At that point, you have three choices: You can go back and resolve to spend more of your free time when you're not at work continuing the work that you've done on sabbatical; you can quit and not go back; or you can go back but set a target date for when you will quit.

Or, you can negotiate for reduced hours at work, or do some or all of your work at home. Working for your company at home—either through telecommunications or by doing work that doesn't require interaction with other people—is becoming more and more popular as businesses begin to yield to the wishes of employees. When most people work part of the time at home, they become much more efficient because they're not constantly interrupted by meetings, colleagues, and clients dropping in, or by a ringing telephone. The social contact of two or three days in the office each week will suffice for many people.

Increased efficiency at work means you'll have more hours to pursue your own projects, not to mention the freedom you have working at home, while you continue to pull in a salary and benefits. This might be the best way for some people to return to work.

Then again, you might just have to accept the fact that you have to go back, and the party's over. You'll find, however, that work will never be the same after a sabbatical, no matter what you decide to do, since on a sabbatical you were able to discover what you are capable of accomplishing—something that is rarely seen in normal workaday life.

THE SABBATICAL FILE

For Chuck Woodbury of Grass Valley, California, his year-long sabbatical helped him to start a business that turned out to fit him like a glove. In the past, he'd worked as a newspaper reporter, a public relations specialist, a freelancer, and he had also owned a small community newspaper. In the summer of 1987, he applied for a job as public information officer at a local college. He knew he had a good chance of getting the job because he had already been filling in at the position for a while.

Although on the surface he thought this was what he wanted, deep down he knew it wasn't. "I'd work on some freelance publicity accounts for a while, but I knew this wasn't really what I wanted to do," he said. So he'd sneak out every so often and hit the road, just traveling around for a week or two, and write a magazine article about his trip. He wasn't making much money, but he was having fun. Once he got out on the road, he'd think, "This is what I really want to do." But his sensible side would counter, telling him he could do well in his business if he hung out a sign and got some steady clients. The frivolous side would retort, "Yeah, but you know you don't like to be in one place all the time, and besides, that would mean that you'd have all these people telling you what to do."

So he sold his newspaper and planned to take two years off to travel out the west in his motor home, which he purchased especially for this purpose. He had a small cottage in Sacramento that served as his home base; he'd travel for four months and then come back for two before heading out again. The purpose of his sabbatical was to live modestly on about $25,000 a year, sell some magazine articles, and find something he really wanted to do, a notion that had been nagging at him for a long time. During his time off, he reread parts of the journal he had kept since 1977. The recurring theme was his desire to get away from where he lived to expand his world.

So he took off. "I knew that if I had a year or two to get out and roam around, that I could figure something out," he said. "Through many lonely nights of sitting in a campground and walking around, I knew that if I gave my brain a chance to wander around a bit, I'd find something."

After he'd been on the road for about a year, he was in Wyoming when he found his answer. It came to him in a flash: He would publish and edit a newspaper called *Out West*, which would be an informal travelogue of Woodbury's ramblings. He headed for home the next day and had the first issue written and published in just six weeks. In 1993, he had 8,000 subscribers all over the country who he says are as unlike his PR clients as they can get. "Before, I had a few clients telling me what to do. Now I have 8,000 subscribers who don't tell me much of anything, except to keep doing what I'm doing. If I hadn't taken the year off, I would have never come up with the idea for the paper because I wouldn't have spent the time out there on the road, where I was relaxed enough so that the ideas just flowed."

He adds that it was wonderful to not work and to know he could still pay his bills every month. Although he'd always worked for himself, he never before had the time to write and to think—and to do it at his own pace.

"Basically, *Out West* is all the things that I've done in my whole life since I first got into journalism in college," he said. "And when I got the idea for the paper, I found that I already had the hats to do it."

Woodbury says that in a way, his year off has never really come to an end. He says that his job is almost 95 percent pure pleasure, and he adds that he receives several letters each week from people in their seventies and eighties congratulating him on publishing the paper.

"They all say that they wanted to do something like what I'm doing years ago, but they didn't because they didn't have the guts."

Ending Your Sabbatical Early

It may be hard to believe, but there are actually some people out there who decide to return to the office early. In some cases, they find that they just aren't able to learn to let go and enjoy the sensation of being untethered from the office. Others may have become disenchanted with their projects and are either unable or unwilling to retool them in midstream. Then again, some people who plan to spend their sabbatical just hanging out around the house find that this isn't for them; they miss the office, the people, and their work.

Joyce Lipton, an attorney with a law firm in Uniondale, New York, maintains that the position of her firm toward a female lawyer going on maternity leave depends largely on the attitude of her supervising partner. "I was lucky, since the head of my department understood and didn't care," she said. "But there were some partners in the firm who took it as a personal insult and an act of disloyalty if one of their attorneys became pregnant. They felt the women weren't good employees and were not doing what was best for the department."

Even though Lipton enjoyed having 11 weeks off maternity leave in the summer of 1992, she felt disconnected from the firm and even went back two weeks earlier than she had anticipated. "After you've been at a job for ten years, when you're away and don't know what's going on on a day-to-day basis, you feel a little out of touch and out of control," she said. "I missed the office, in a different way than when I've been on vacation and didn't miss the office. I wondered what was going on, and I stayed in touch."

Lipton works in litigation, and her leave coincided with summer, which is slow season in the courts. She arranged to have her trials adjourn in the last months of her pregnancy and start up again in the beginning of September so she could come back to continue the trials. If it was necessary to do any additional work or question witnesses in the interim, another person at the firm could take over since the work for each case was distributed in a fairly informal manner among the members of her team.

Lipton adds that some of the partners at the firm are skittish about attorneys taking leaves for any reason because a couple of women who went on maternity leave never came back, and a man who was granted a personal leave of absence also didn't return.

If you decide to cut short your sabbatical and go back early, be clear about why you're doing it. Don't just tell people around you that you thought that doing nothing was dumb, or that your project just wasn't right for you. Any sabbatical can be altered so that it's what you want it to be at any time during your break. If it scares you to have that much time off, admit it and face it, or do something else where you can benefit.

Getting permission to drop out so you can do what you want to for a while is a great advantage that most people don't get. Don't waste it.

What If It's Not Working?

It's a hard thing to admit that the wonderful break that you scrimped and planned for somehow isn't working out like you thought it would. Should you keep plodding on and hope that it gets better? Or, should you scrap your plans and switch to something totally different?

Of course, you should realize that, as I mentioned earlier in this chapter, your sabbatical is going to look quite different when it's over from what you had expected. If what you're doing doesn't feel quite right, you should ask yourself if your initial expectations for your sabbatical were too high. Most of us have had a vacation that didn't live up to what we had expected. In that case, you try and figure out what went wrong, write it off, and try again next year.

With a sabbatical, however, while the approach is the same, you actually have less time to figure out why it's not working. After all, you don't want to waste the rest of your time off troubleshooting. To determine where things have gone awry, ask yourself the following questions:

- [ ] Did you over- or underschedule your time?
- [ ] Did you expect too much?
- [ ] Did it take you a while to get used to being off? Is your sabbatical half over and you're only now hitting your stride?
- [ ] Did you pick something to do based not on your own desires, but on somebody else's? Were you wrong in what you initially thought you wanted?
- [ ] Does your sabbatical seem too much like work?

If any of your answers to the above questions indicate that you should revamp your sabbatical, then do it. Maybe you've gone off on a tangent and haven't come back yet. Sometimes, just like in real life, people on sabbatical find it easier to concentrate on one aspect of their leave. We tend to be specialists, after all, both at work and at leisure. Would it be to your benefit to continue in this vein? Or does focusing on just one part really defeat the whole purpose of your leave?

Being on sabbatical means that you have to take a broader look at yourself and recognize both your strengths and shortcomings. If you took your sabbatical for the wrong reasons, you might even have to scrap your entire plan and spend the rest of your time off doing what you really want to do, whether it's lying in a hammock or learning how to sail.

In sum, if you're having trouble, it's especially important to quickly evaluate what's gone wrong so you can retool and concentrate on what will make you feel at the end that your sabbatical was worth it.

What Will Your Sabbatical Look Like?

As I've said earlier, it's difficult to know exactly what your time off will be like until you're already there. In your notebook, write down your thoughts and actions to the following questions so that you are prepared for them. Then, when you're on sabbatical and the unexpected arises, you can refer to these answers in order to compare your fantasies with reality and adjust your sabbatical accordingly.

- ☐ What are some of the expectations that you have about your sabbatical?
- ☐ Are you prepared to switch gears if your sabbatical starts to disappoint you?
- ☐ What external motivations will you set up to keep you going?

☐ How will you maintain contact with friends and family at home if you're traveling?

☐ What will you do if you have to cut your sabbatical short?

BRAINSTORM: On paper describe your perfect sabbatical day.

THE SABBATICAL FILE

Anne Edmonds, librarian at Mount Holyoke College, took a sabbatical from her job during the second half of 1976. She was approached by the United States/South Africa Leader Exchange Program, or USSALEP, an international Quaker organization, to work at a black university in South Africa for several months. At that time, Edmonds had been at Mount Holyoke for 12 years, and there were no provisions for non-teaching faculty to take a sabbatical. She approached the president of the college about taking a paid leave. He told her if the library could operate smoothly without hiring a replacement, then he'd grant her request. She began her leave in August of 1976.

She worked as a consultant with the library director at the University of the North in a small town called Turfloop, five hours north of Johannesburg by car. She spent most of her time there working with the library staff, but she was also able to fit in some side trips, which included traveling with some of the black staff to their tribal homeland areas. While Edmonds was in South Africa, race relations were very tense, because she was visiting just after the Soweto riots, and many of the students at the University of the North had been rioting as well. Some of the more radical students were trying to shut down the University while she was there, and she says that sometimes it was difficult to know who was on which side. Although it took some time, Edmonds says that she was eventually able to earn the trust and support of the entire library staff.

While she was away, Edmonds wrote long letters about her trip and sent them back to the staff at the Mount Holyoke library. Because of her isolation and the political situation at the time, Edmonds said that she learned to be self-reliant, and the letters she wrote back kept her in touch with the library at home. Her colleagues wrote back as well, which she says helped her feel less isolated.

One of the Mount Holyoke staffers who wrote back was Elaine Trehub, archives librarian, who eventually went on her own sabbatical from April to August of 1992. As a result of Edmonds's successful sabbatical, the college drew up a leave policy for librarians in May of 1990. The librarians and administration didn't want their sabbatical to have the publishing requirements of a traditional sabbatical. Instead, they instituted a specific policy statement that would require a librarian to produce a tangible project based on her sabbatical that would be approved by the dean and by Edmonds in advance. The sabbatical program is geared towards librarians at a certain level who have been with the college for seven years. They can apply for up to four months paid leave. But, says Edmonds, time off can be granted only for a specific project related to the library sciences. "A librarian can't just go off for four months on holiday," she says.

When Trehub went on her sabbatical, she had been working at the college for 19 years. As an archivist at a women's college, she'd become interested in the archival resources available for women's studies, and she made this the focus of her sabbatical. She wanted to study similar resources that were available in the United Kingdom, particularly England. She chose England because she believed that the similarities in culture and language would facilitate her study. She visited several colleges including Oxford, Cambridge, and the University of London.

Trehub was the first librarian to take a leave under the new program at Mount Holyoke, and she says that more librarians at the college will take leaves in the future. "I came back with a very different sense of self, and a very different sense of context in which our collection operates," she said. She adds that one of the things she enjoyed most about her leave was being able to visit other libraries as a patron and not as a librarian or archivist.

Leave Your Ego at the Door

If you've held a prestigious well-paying job for a number of years and get lots of respect and some envy from your colleagues, it's easy to, as they say, start to believe your own press releases and get the erroneous notion that everything you touch will turn to gold.

If you fall into this category, the most important lesson you may learn from your sabbatical is humility. Although everyone is good at something, no one is good at everything, and there's no better way to find that out than on a sabbatical. If you're using your time off to learn how to do something you've always wanted to do, but never had the chance to before, be prepared to take a lot of baby steps in the beginning.

Culture Shock

If you're going to be traveling by yourself or even with a companion in a foreign country, the exposure to different cultures can be very enlightening.

Even though Rosella Sabatini traveled with a friend on her three-month trip in Asia and Japan, she did spend a couple of days on her own in Malaysia at a primitive island resort because her friend had made other travel arrangements. "It was a bit scary, because it was early on in the trip and I wasn't used to being this strange foreigner," she said. "I was always stopping traffic when I crossed the street, and people were always staring at me. It was odd to be the minority in another country. I don't think I ever got used to that."

It took a week for her to get over the initial shock of traveling in countries where living conditions were so primitive, even for tourists. Sabatini would occasionally splurge by taking a hotel room with air conditioning.

For two women traveling alone in countries that were mostly Muslim, being hassled by the men was a common occurrence. She says she thinks that the men stare in part because they're so restricted in their own lives and in the way they protect their own women, and also because they have crazy ideas about western women and assume the worst. "We were in Thailand, and having a bad travel day, when this teenage boy grabbed my arm," she said. "A lot of times they saw the white skin and wanted to see what it felt like. But that day, I turned around and slapped him across the face. I couldn't believe that I reacted that way, and I felt sorry for him, and we ran off." She says she learned that usually the best thing for women to do was to completely ignore the barrage of comments.

Although it helps to know a little bit of the language when you're traveling in a foreign country, it isn't always necessary. Rosella Sabatini spoke only English, but Anna, the friend she was traveling with, knew how to speak a little Cantonese, as well as how to write in the language.

If you're traveling in countries in the third world, it's usually possible to find someone who speaks English, even in remote villages. This is because the people are poor and rely so heavily on the tourist trade that the natives tend to make an effort with foreigners. In any case, it is probably a good idea to invest in a language course or tapes before your trip if you're planning to spend a good deal of time overseas.

Trial by Fire

Like Sabatini, Kathy and Rob Merrill, who traveled around the world with a backpack, say that their lives on the road were a complete turnaround from their previous ones. "When we were traveling, our decisions boiled down to where are we going to sleep, what are we going to eat, and where are we going to go next?" said Kathy. "It focused on primitive needs, and life was very simple. We never had reservations anywhere, and sometimes we really got caught up in the logistics of it all. For instance, sometimes cashing a check turned out to take up our whole day."

Living this way for nine months isn't for every couple, but for the Merrills, it strengthened their relationship considerably. Because they only had each other to entertain, they relied on each other, sometimes to a fault. "Kathy likes to say that we spent a lot of time recounting each other's histories back to the most primitive memories," says Rob. He adds that he thinks there were maybe ten hours when they were apart for the whole trip.

"We look at how the trip bonded us, especially when we look at friends who haven't had that kind of breaking-away experience," says Rob. "They don't have a sense of what they've missed. I think that couples who haven't had a trial by fire don't cling together during a crisis. We know a number of people who have divorced, and it seems tragic that it may be because their relationship never went through any tough times."

9

Reentering the Real World

The Immediate Reentry

It's time to go back to work, and it's a good bet that for most people, the end comes far too soon. There's usually an inevitable letdown and adjustment period if you're going back to work; and if you've decided to quit your job, the absence of a safety net can be harrowing. Just as you could plan your sabbatical down to the smallest detail and still not fully know what to expect, your preparation for reentering the real world will work up to a point.

The day before she was scheduled to return to the *Boston Globe*, Diane Nottle said that she spent most of the day crying. "I really didn't want to go back," she said. "I found that the Globe hadn't changed much in terms of operations or its outlook, but I had changed, and I didn't want to fall back into my old patterns."

Despite her best intentions, she did return to some of her old habits. Although she switched to a different assignment on the same desk, which allowed her a little more independence than before, she was still unhappy with her job. She stayed at the paper one more year before leaving to freelance, and in 1988, she moved to New York and joined the *New York Times* as an editor on the cultural news desk.

"Coming back was like hitting the brakes," comments Nick Leeming on his year off. Although he admits that he was glad to be settling down again to school, he says that traveling all over the world was more exhausting than he had imagined. His readjustment went smoothly, however, because he came back in time to have a couple of weeks to reacclimate himself before school started. A couple of years after his sabbatical, he spent a summer between semesters working on a ranch in Montana. When he returned to school, he was surprised to find out how easy it was to slip back into being Nick Leeming from Tufts University. "In a way, it was scary," he says. "It was almost as if nothing had changed."

But he's changed. Nick considered himself a pretty up-tight person, but after his year-long sabbatical, he says he learned how to take things more in stride. "Now, if things aren't going right, I can sit down and work through it, or shrug it off," he says. "While I was traveling around and having to deal with problems on my own every day, I gained a feeling of taking everything in stride."

Scheduling Downtime

Leeming and others who've taken time off say it's a good idea to plan for some extra time between your arrival home and when you're due back at work, or else the shock just might be too great. Alisa Wechsler went back to work immediately after she returned from Yaddo so that she could pay off some of the debts she had incurred while she was gone. But because her sabbatical was so intense, and her everyday life was so different, she discovered that her return was particularly difficult, especially since she had to dive into five and six ten-hour shifts a week.

"There's no way I could have padded the shock of returning to my old life," she said. "It was like culture shock." Wechsler had grown so accustomed to the other people at the colony, that when she came home, she felt very lonely. She says that it took about a month before she was able to start working on her art again. She was also sad to leave the security and the space she was working in and have to pack up everything that she had created there.

In the first few weeks after her sabbatical ended, she viewed her job as the one obstacle that kept her from doing her work, because she had grown so used to spending the whole day doing nothing but her art. "At Yaddo, my job was to get up and do my work, and back home, my regular job kept me from doing it," she said.

Her resentment eventually wore off, and she says that she spends more time working on her art now than she did before she took time off. She's already planning for her next sabbatical at Yaddo or another colony.

If you can manage it, arrange to have some time to decompress after your sabbatical.

- ☐ Come back a few days early and spend the time relaxing.
- ☐ Wind down during the last week by spending an hour less each day on your sabbatical project.
- ☐ Take a real vacation. Go someplace and play tourist to unwind from your sabbatical and prepare for your return to work.

Culture Shock

Although Rosella Sabatini wasn't returning to the same job, she was still unhappy when she came back from three months of traveling throughout Asia. She had arranged to return a month before starting graduate school and said that she felt disoriented for a week after her return.

"After I got back, I remember going to Wall Street to visit friends at my old job, and I got off the subway during lunchtime and I couldn't remember how to walk with the crowd," says Sabatini, who grew up in New York. "People were walking around me and tripping over me, and I was overwhelmed by how fast everybody moved."

Also, Sabatini, whose size is closer to smaller, thinner Asians than Americans, commented, "I couldn't help noticing how fat Americans are. Everyone where I visited overseas was my size, and I came home and people were big again."

Since her sabbatical, she says that she tries to take her vacations all at once so she can take trips that at least echo her extended time off. "I always assume that there will be another trip like this, and I'm always looking for the next opportunity," she says. In 1993, she spent three weeks in Morocco. "And if I change jobs again, I'll try to work it out so I have another long break."

What If You Don't Go Back?

Through all of the pleading, bargaining, and cajoling you had to do with your boss to get the time off to take your sabbatical, implicit was the understanding that you'd come back when it was over. But what if you've changed your mind? In chapter 1, quitting a job was listed as one of the top ten myths about sabbaticals, but it does happen some of the time. After the freedom and new possibilities that you tasted during your sabbatical, going back to your old job might be the last thing you want.

What should you do? It depends on how badly you want out. For instance, if your boss had informed you that it was company policy to pay back the cash value of any benefits or salary you received during your leave if you didn't return, and you had quickly initialed that clause in your agreement because you wanted your boss to sign before he changed his mind, if you have a substantial trust fund, then it won't matter.

Most of us, however, would give great pause to paying it back, even if the thought of spending one more day in the office would make you nauseous. If you've already agreed to start another job when you were due to return to the old one, you might ask your new employer to strike a deal with your soon-to-be-ex-employer. But don't count on it. Even the asking might sour your relationship with your new boss. Besides, this is your problem.

If you've signed a piece of paper that includes a provision for the payback of benefits or salary in the event that you don't return, you're legally obligated to pay back the money. If, however, you want to take the risk and hope that your former company decides not to come after you, go ahead. Keep in mind, though, that salaries can be garnished and liens placed on homes in order to satisfy debts. Fortunately, agreements like these occur mostly in large corporations and not the majority of small businesses.

Barring this possible setback, how should you inform your boss that you don't plan to return? I think the best way is with a face-to-face meeting several weeks before you're due back. In that meeting, be as honest as you can and give your reasons why you don't plan to return. It's probably not necessary to go into great detail, and you also might be surprised to find out that your boss isn't interested in why you want to leave.

To lessen the blow to your boss and the office, you might offer to come back for a month to smooth the way for your successor and help with the transition, but this is solely at your discretion. It depends on the type of job you have, how quickly a replacement can be found, and the type of boss you have. If you don't want to totally burn your bridges, it's probably a good idea to take a deep breath and do whatever you have to do for a period of time to remain in the good graces of your boss and the company. In any case, if you're definitely going to leave your job at the end of your sabbatical, try to remain on good terms with the company.

THE SABBATICAL FILE

"When I went back to my job after my leave, I wasn't too happy about starting back with the same dull routine, which is the reason I had originally gotten into photography," says Evelyn McClure, who took a month-long leave under Wells Fargo's Personal Growth Leave.

On her return she worked for Crocker Bank, which Wells Fargo had acquired in 1986. The merger had resulted in downsizing, and her job changed along with her boss, who ended up being a man she didn't get along with. Shortly after she returned from her leave, she began to plan her next sabbatical. "My first leave gave me a taste of what it was like to have time off, and so I decided to do it again, but this time on my terms," she said.

After spending 25 years living in city apartments, McClure and her husband bought a house in rural Sonoma County, 50 miles north of San Francisco. For Evelyn, this proved to be the beginning of the end of her job at the bank. For the first year, she and her family—she has a teenage daughter—commuted to the house on weekends. A year later, they moved to the house full-time.

She spent one more year commuting to her job in San Francisco, an hour-and-a-half bus ride each way, before she made the break. Since Evelyn's husband was retired, he was happy that she'd be home full-time.

"It really hasn't been a big change for me, since I've been gearing myself towards doing this for so long," says McClure. "When I quit to take this time off, I was afraid that I really wouldn't do anything, that I'd fall into a malaise and not accomplish anything." To stave this off, she started taking photography classes and working as a volunteer photographer with the local historical society. She's not sure how long she'll be away from work, or even if she'll ever go back. "I don't know if I'll eventually miss working, because things as they stand financially are pretty tight," she says. "We have enough for the basics and a little left over, but not enough to splurge, so if I can do it, I'd like to stay out as long as possible."

A Difficult Readjustment

Sometimes people on leave get so caught up with what they're doing that they start to delude themselves about what they're going to do when it's over and they have to return to work. You may have watched other people come back from leave and think you have it figured out so you don't have to worry about returning. Be forewarned: It will still catch you by surprise.

As the archives librarian at Mount Holyoke College, Elaine Trehub had watched many academics come back from their sabbaticals. "I think they all come back and immediately fall into a deep depression," she said. "They'll come back and be incredibly restless." Since she was only going to be gone for four months, she thought she would be able to jump right back in and get back to work with no side effects.

She was wrong. When she first returned to work, she

was incredibly energized, and she immediately began to write about her project for a professional journal, as was required by the college. But that effort faded as she began to readjust to the real world. Almost a year after her return, she still hadn't completed her article, which greatly frustrated her. As more time passed, she found that her reluctance to finish her article began to detract from the advantages of the sabbatical as a whole.

"My sabbatical was an unreal world for me, just as it is for the people who go away from here for a year," she said. "And that requires some readjustment, but I can't tell you what kind. The interesting thing was that I didn't feel it as soon as I came back, but later."

As the one-year anniversary of her departure date approached, her anxiety increased and her adjustment worsened. "As April approached, I thought about the fact that last April I was leaving on my trip," she said. "And this time last year I was at Durham, and so on. I relived it all the way." This continued throughout each of the four corresponding months of the following year, but interestingly, her tension began to fade as the one-year anniversary of her return date neared. "It's been a very funny feeling, comparing this summer with last summer," she said. "I'm surprised at the hold it still has on me."

Back Home: Learning to Be Comfortable Again

We're creatures of habit. We become used to living under a certain standard of living conditions, and we balk if we're asked to change. But then we become comfortable with that change, which then makes it hard to change yet again—until we grow used to it, that is.

Like Rosella Sabatini, Jordan Schaffel discovered that he

had some unusual adjustments to make once he returned from his year-long trip around the world. "I flew back to Florida from Tahiti, and my parents both met me and were wearing T-shirts that said, 'What a long strange trip it's been.' It took me two or three weeks to acclimate to being back. I didn't know what I was going to do next, so I got a job shortly after I returned."

Schaffel said that the most difficult part of coming back to the states after living out of a backpack for the better part of a year was learning to become comfortable with what was comfortable again. "I saw the world differently when I got back," he said. "I was used to being uncomfortable, so I didn't think that I needed all my luxuries to be happy, and I still feel that way to this day."

He stayed at his parents' house for a couple of weeks until his tenants moved out of his house and believes this helped him to adjust to being back, because it allowed him to slowly segue back into his own world. He thinks it would be a good idea for other people to arrange their home and life so they could settle right in and decompress from the sabbatical for a while. Schaffel suggests tacking three or four weeks of downtime to the end of a sabbatical to lessen the strain.

When You're at 33 RPMs and the World's at 78

When you're working at a job in a company where every employee gets a sabbatical, you're a little better prepared for coming back, since there are so many test cases wandering the halls. "There's a rule of thumb that says you shouldn't come back for a full week after you return from a trip," says Kevin Kean of Tandem. "I think that's rational, because there's an intensity level at work that you're simply not going to be prepared to face." He tells of a friend who came back from his sabbatical just as Kean was starting to ship a new product. Kean was putting in 14-hour days, and the friend just wandered in and said, "Hi! Sit down, take a break." Kean looked at him like he was crazy.

"It does take some time to get back on this moving sidewalk that's going a hundred miles an hour," he said. "It helps to have some idea of what you're going to come back to, since it's an emotional, and in some ways, a physical adjustment."

Before he left, Kean worried about whether he'd be forgotten at the office. "How is it that I can find myself working 12 hours a day, 6 days a week, and I can walk away from it for 8 weeks and the company doesn't disappear?" he queries. "If you can come to grips with that question, then you think, 'I wonder if my job will be there when I get back.'"

Whenever these concerns surfaced during his sabbatical, Kean said he comforted himself by envisioning that his "In" basket would be six feet high when he returned. He and his wife returned from their trip to Europe a few days before Kean was due back at work. After about a week, he said, he was back to normal.

An Unwelcome Return

Sometimes, even after the benefits of a sabbatical, overcoming the resistance of your colleagues once you return to the office can be difficult. What can you do to overcome this resistance? The primary thing is to show your colleagues and supervisors that you intend to stay committed to the company and do the same amount of work that you did before. You may find that you've become more efficient in your tasks, so that work takes less time and you have more time for your family and other interests.

Your co-workers, however, might be incredibly jealous of what you've been able to pull off. The best thing to do is to gradually win them over to your side, pointing out instances where you're as committed as they are, even though you got to be away from the office for a while. Suggest that they begin to plan their own sabbatical, and offer to serve as their mentor. Ask them what they would do if they had six months to spend in whatever way they wanted. Bring them through the steps that you took, and give them time to realize that they can take a sabbatical, too. Help to make them aware that even though it's scary, they should take the chance, because the rewards are much greater than the risks.

But when you go back to work, you shouldn't necessarily see your return to the *real* world as going back to the *old* world. "After a sabbatical, it's important to create a new set of parameters, even within the same firm," says Nella Barkley. Take for example lawyers, who've returned to their firms after sabbaticals and instead of practicing corporate law, have gone on to become managing partners or else investigate a different kind of law. Or doctors, who decide that they're tired of practicing medicine and would rather become involved in the administration of HMOs. Says Barkley, "The idea is to reconfigure your work around your skills and desires."

Just Another Day

For some people, returning to work is just another day; no big deal. Steve Seigal, who worked for IBM, said that the adjustment he had to make after he returned from his first sabbatical wasn't as tough as he had imagined it to be. He said that the first day back at work wasn't one of the more significant events in his life, but he did have a sense of being welcomed back, comparing it to seeing his old friends at a high school reunion.

"I don't think there's anything you can do to prepare for going back to work," he said. "If you're going to sign up to take a class, and you've never taken the class before, you just show up and begin."

Bob Sheeran reacted the same way. After he and his wife returned from a paid 14-week sabbatical in Europe, he went from a business meeting in New York right back to the office. "We had accomplished what we set out to do," he said. "I was ready to go back."

The Crash

More likely people are unhappy to be back and fight tooth and nail to hold onto the benefits they gained during their leave, despite incredible pressures to the contrary.

Although she initially didn't want to come back at all, when Cindy Mason returned from leading her first European bicycle trip, she said she was on a roll for the first few weeks at work. Then came the crash. "I was on such a high from doing bike trips, that when reality finally hit, it hit hard," she said. Three weeks after she returned, she became depressed. "It was hard to get back into the routine of work again knowing that all I wanted to do was move on. I liked my job and was good at it, but I think I was just bored. I have never been bored doing bike trips."

There's not much you can do to soften the blow that you'll probably feel once you return to work. Some people ease out of their sabbaticals by going back to work a few days a week or a few hours a day at first. The important thing is to stay in touch with the things you accomplished on your time off, which will help make the transition back to real life less of a shock to your system.

What's Next?

Sabbatical Postmortem

After your sabbatical is over—either the next day or after a few weeks, when you've had some time to reflect—it's a good idea to evaluate your time off. Look at the areas where you met or exceeded your goals as well as the other areas where you would have liked to do a little better.

Why should you evaluate your sabbatical? To see how the time off best suited you. I'm assuming that the subject of your sabbatical is an interest that you plan to pursue long after you return to work. Therefore, it will help you to get an idea if it's worth it to give more of your attention to the areas where you think you fell short, or to decide to just ditch it and concentrate on the parts that you enjoy most and do best.

Doing a postmortem will also help you to plan future sabbaticals. Be honest and answer the following questions in your notebook in as much detail as you want.

1. Do you think you accomplished the main goals of your sabbatical? How so?
2. List the five best things you learned from your sabbatical, and tell how you learned them.
3. List the five things you didn't learn but wanted to. How could you have arranged your sabbatical to place more priority on them?
4. What would you have done differently on your time off, if anything? What would remain the same?
5. What are you going to do with what you've learned?

6. What would you like your next sabbatical to look like? Start planning it now.

Making Your Return Special

The last day of your sabbatical is both an end and a beginning. Your time off is over, but now you begin to realize how much more you're capable of doing, and you can bring that to bear on your everyday life.

Some people think they're going to have an easy time adjusting when they return; others don't even think about it. Still others know they're going to have trouble, and they plan to deal with it far in advance.

Even if you've only been away for a month, your return should be cause for a celebration of what you were able to accomplish and what's next for you. If you had time off by yourself, gather your friends and family together a couple of days before your sabbatical is over to tell them what you've learned and what you plan to do.

Pat Newlin knew that she would have a difficult time when she returned to her public relations business after spending two months in Paris, so she asked one of her employees to orchestrate a reentry party for her the night she returned, with all her employees present. "I felt it was the best way to get all of the 'Wow, how was it?' out of the way, and done in a friendly social atmosphere instead of me having to do it ten times the next day."

You should also be prepared to help others plan their own sabbaticals. As Jordan Schaffel said, "I promised myself when my sabbatical was over that I'd do whatever I could to help other people who wanted to take time off, too."

If you took a family sabbatical, take the last week or so to wind down. It's a good idea for all family members to write down their own postmortems. Take turns reading them out loud, and then take some time to talk about what you've gained as a family. When the Babbitt family returned to Maine after spending the better part of a year on boat, they found that the closer bonds they had formed while they were away began to unravel almost immediately upon their return home.

"Coming back was a letdown," says Jane Babbitt. "We had so many details to attend to, opening the house up, looking for work, and reestablishing ourselves in the community, that the girls were complaining that the family was splitting apart because we weren't as close as we had been on the boat." Their solution was to move to another town, further up the Maine coast, and for Tom to find a job where he worked fewer hours than his previous position.

If you plan to return to your job, be aware that some people spend the last days of their sabbaticals crying hysterically. Others spend it quietly, trying to gear up for returning to a pace that is probably much different from what they've grown accustomed to.

In any case, and in keeping with the theme of your sabbatical, do something that you wouldn't have done before to celebrate the fact that you were indeed able to have a successful sabbatical. You might start by setting a target date for your next one.

Changing Your Existing Job at Your Present Company

When your sabbatical ends, you return to your job as planned, but you find that it doesn't quite fit the way it used to. You've changed but it hasn't, and you find yourself thinking about quitting.

Don't jump yet. If you're happy with your company, and they've been pleased with your work, you might approach them about switching to another job in the same or a different department.

Maybe you want less responsibility and/or fewer hours. Although some of your co-workers may look at you in wonder, you should maintain that this is what you want for yourself, and it doesn't matter if you're making less money or carry a less prestigious title. If it's possible to create a new position, combining the best of your current job with some new responsibilities you'd like to carry, maybe you could pass some of your old duties on to a colleague or assistant.

If there's nothing available right away, do what you have to do to get your work done while remaining true to what you ultimately want to do with the company within the context of your new outlook.

Going into Business for Yourself

If you are considering becoming an entrepreneur, what you should realize is that this may be the best time you'll ever have to start a business. For one, you're riding high on your capabilities and have a lot of energy that will, in all probability, be sorely sapped if you return to your old lifestyle. In addition, you may have developed new contacts during your sabbatical who know you only from this upbeat phase of your life. Most likely they'll be willing to help you get started, no matter what it takes. People from your pre-sabbatical days, no matter how impressed they are that you were able to pull it off, may be skeptical about your ability to get a business off the ground.

Forget about them. Surround yourself and rely on people who believe you're capable of anything. This is probably the most important predictor of success as an entrepreneur. And remember, if you wait any longer to start, it just may be too late.

Changing Your Lifestyle

It may be presumptuous of me to say this, but I think that everyone who takes time off from her normal routine finds that her lifestyle changes to some extent. Whether it's as little as changing your perspective that there's more to life than working, to deciding that you're going to chuck it all and use your savings to build a house and become totally self-sufficient, it's impossible not to become affected in some way. Even if you do return to the same job at the same crazed pace you held before your sabbatical, you'll at least be able to realize that it's a choice you make and not something that you're pushed into by forces beyond your control.

Families that go on sabbatical together inevitably discover that they become much closer during their time away. Then, after they return to their old lives, it's frequently the kids who complain almost immediately that they don't feel like a family anymore. In reality, it's their old version of family that doesn't fit their new lives anymore.

If you want to change your lifestyle in any way, you have to map out a plan, timetable, and budget, just like you did when you planned your sabbatical. Like your sabbatical plan, there may be unforeseen complications that arise. Unlike your sabbatical plan, however, executing a complete lifestyle change must assume a different tone and tempo, since you're looking for a permanent change. In addition, in your postsabbatical glow, it's possible that you'll see that anything is feasible, and, as a result, you may overestimate what you'll be able to achieve and underestimate how long it will take. Although it may be difficult not to burst out of the starting gate, try to err on the side of conservatism and build in some extra time as a buffer. That way, if you finish ahead of time, you'll be pleasantly surprised.

A Sample Plan

Because a sabbatical is such a common fantasy, and is also one that I was able to accomplish a number of years ago, I'll describe how one person with a corporate job and a family can manage to move from the suburbs to the country and start his own business.

Michael Rosen has been married to the same woman for 12 years and working as an architect for the same company for 15. His wife, Marcia, is VP in charge of marketing at a computer software company. They have two kids, a boy who's seven, and a girl, ten. They are happy with their jobs, but they're beginning to look at what else they could do, since they'd like to run their own business together, and they dream of living in the country. They also have a sizable investment portfolio that they're ready to cash in to invest in their business. Eventually they'd like to run a country inn but think they need some experience first. What should they do?

1.   Before they invest in a country inn, the Rosens should make sure that they're right for the business. They should either work at an established inn for at least a year once they move to a rural area, or buy a house with a few extra bedrooms so they can open a bed-and-breakfast and test the waters. If they opt for the B&B, either one or both will need to work at another job to support the family. At best, such a bed-and-breakfast arrangement should only be considered supplementary income. Either way, the Rosens should consider this warning: Playing host to strangers is a lot harder than it looks.

2. The Rosens should make sure they have enough money saved up to live for two years, even if they decide to work outside the house. Good-paying jobs in most rural areas are hard to find, and even if the Rosens have income from the B&B and some freelance work, business planners suggest that entrepreneurs budget for twice the expenses they think they'll need for the first couple of years in order to establish themselves until the business becomes more steady.

3. Before the Rosens leave their companies, they should try to line up some freelance work in advance, whether from the businesses they're leaving or from their competitors. Investing in a powerful computer system, fax, modem, and other office equipment and supplies goes without saying.

4. Country caveat: No one can learn everything there is to know about rural living by subscribing to a magazine. Although the Rosens believe they've had the "advantages" of living in a more populated area, they shouldn't consider themselves self-appointed missionaries whose purpose is to point out to their new neighbors the errors of their uninformed, backwater ways. The Rosens should take care to be humble and respectful of their neighbors' lifestyles. I guarantee they'll learn much more from the people around them than from magazines.

Drawing Up a Timetable to Change Your Lifestyle

As with planning a sabbatical, it's a good idea to use a year as a starting point when planning your move to the country or making another type of lifestyle change. If you need more time, or are more anxious, speed up or stretch out this timetable to meet your needs. And if you're ambitious, it is possible to combine this timetable with the sabbatical planning schedule and kill two birds with one stone. I use starting a bed-and-breakfast as an example, although the ideas described in this schedule can be adapted to any kind of lifestyle change.

Your Timetable for a Lifestyle Change

12 months in advance

Start scouting out the area where you want to live. Put your house on the market and start house hunting. Also start thinking about the kind of work you want to do once you move.

10 months in advance

Start investigating the things you'll need to run your business or get the job you need. Subscribe to the local newspapers and magazines, and talk to other people who have already been living in the area for a while.

8 months in advance

If you can manage it financially, buy a house in the country now. Start to live there part-time and prepare it in order to receive guests when you move there full-time.

6 months in advance

If you plan to work in your new area, in addition to running the B&B, it's not too early to investigate future openings, especially at inns.

4 months in advance

If you still plan to open your B&B when you first move to the country, you should start now to apply for all of the necessary permits, from fire and health inspections to registering with the state as a hospitality business. You should also start to get to know other B&B owners and innkeepers in the area, who will likely pass on extra business to you when they're full. Draw up your business plan.

(Continued)

> (Continued)
>
> *2 months in advance*
>
> Start confirming future work assignments, and begin to market the B&B. If you've been offered a job, confirm that it will start shortly after you move in.
>
> *1 month in advance*
>
> Sell everything you don't need. Start packing. Make sure all your old jobs are tied up so you have a week or two of packing and organizing before you move.
>
> *1 to 2 weeks in advance*
>
> Switch your mail over, confirm your moving arrangements, and make sure all the utilities are set to be turned on at your new place.

An Aside

"I can live anywhere," I used to tell anyone who would listen. And so I could. But that didn't mean I wanted to. Here's a case in point: Back in 1988 I had finally had it with New York, where I had been living for seven years. Although I had talked about moving to the country for several years, I always chickened out and decided to hang in for just a while longer. After all, it was the unknown that I was thinking about jumping into, much like a sabbatical is for you at this point.

Anyway, after having one of those I-lived-through-it stories that New Yorkers love to tell—"I was on the D train on New Year's Eve in 1987 and this guy pulls a knife on this woman cop half his size, and by the time she had radioed for help, he was down on the platform at the Brooklyn Bridge stop doing pushups for her"—I took that as an omen. I moved to Vermont three months later.

Although I had work to do once I was settled, when I

first moved to the country, I spent most of my time learning about the ways the locals lived; their ways were as totally foreign to me as I was to them with my thick accent. In order to cull more information from them, and to not seem like such an outsider, I tried losing my New York accent. It worked.

During those years I spent in New York yearning for the country, I kept telling myself that once I felt established in my business and had enough contacts for steady work, I would move. I lined up several future assignments, and, with the incident on the subway still fresh in my mind, I finally moved in March of 1988.

A funny thing happened once I got there. Being no longer surrounded by the constant and deafening message to strive and work and succeed as I had been in New York, I wasn't as conscientious about following up on my contacts. But something else was going on, too. I was no longer interested in working like I had worked in the city. The slower pace and the encouragement I got to enjoy what was around me was working its influence.

Also, since my expenses were greatly reduced—my monthly rent was now $200 compared to $700 in Brooklyn—I felt like I didn't need to work as hard as I had. This was the beginning of my rural sabbatical, which continues to this day. Today, my share of the mortgage is about the same—$200—but I spend more time playing than working, although in my daydreams and travels I'm constantly on the lookout for ideas or overheard comments that would translate well to the printed page.

After I moved to the country, I changed so much, in fact, that there were periods when I didn't write for months. I could have easily gotten assignments if I wanted to, but again, something else was going on: the drive to enjoy both the country and my life instead of speed past it. For a time, I worked in restaurants so I could pay my bills but still retain my autonomy.

My point is that your value system may well change after your sabbatical ends, and some of the things you couldn't live without before may seem totally superfluous to you now. Consider yourself forewarned.

You Know What You Should Do Now, But . . .

Even though a sabbatical of any length usually ends up changing the person who takes it and shows them a direction they know they should take after they return, sometimes it still takes a long time to act upon it. Mariana Gosnell, who flew across the country for three months, says that she should have left her job with the magazine soon after she returned from her sabbatical, but instead she stayed on for ten more years. Although her time off turned her in the direction of writing books, she says she stayed at the magazine because she wanted to write a book and needed the financial support to get her through it. "It got me out of my regular life, and if I hadn't taken the leave, it might have been hard for me to figure out what my first book would be about," she said, adding that she might have left the magazine sooner if she hadn't gone on sabbatical. "It was a life-changing event," she says, "but it didn't change it soon enough."

She left the magazine in 1988 to freelance. The book about her sabbatical, *Zero Three Bravo*, was published in 1993 by Knopf.

Holding onto What You've Gained

Although you know that you're a different person after your sabbatical, and you vow to live a different life once your sabbatical has ended, especially if you go back to the job you had before, it's very hard not to slip back into your old, sometimes destructive habits. How can you prevent this from happening and still retain all of the good things you've learned from having time off?

First, take the answers you wrote down in your sabbatical postmortem earlier in this chapter and look at the list of things you've gained. If it helps to make a sign and hang it up at work, or put some reminders in a place so that they're never more than arm's length away, do it. This will help you to be aware of when you're slipping, a mental rubber band of sorts around your brain when you find yourself doing or saying the kinds of things that caused you to think about taking time off in the first place.

If you find it's more comfortable for you to work at a slower pace at the office to keep from losing your perspective on what's important, then do it. Make up for the time by being just a little less social; interruptions by co-workers rapidly eat into the efficiency of employees in every industry. On the same note, don't go off in the other direction and consider yourself superior because of the things you learned from having time off. Don't be preachy about your sabbatical. As the cliché goes, people will get it if you live by example.

Take a breather each day—at the office or at home—that in some way reminds you of your sabbatical. This daily reinforcement may be the best way of holding on to what you've got.

10

Just Do It

Most people come back from their first sabbatical or family leave already thinking about their next one, but what's next for you is to plan and nail down your first one. Over the course of this book, you may have thought about what you'd like to do, planned it, figured out how you're going to finance it and inform the boss, and even set the date for your return. But there's still one thing left to do—Actually do it.

Most of the people who've taken sabbaticals have one piece of advice: Just do it. "Just do it," says Ben Burns. "Don't think about what's going to happen when you get back. If you feel secure enough at the moment to do what you want to do, then do it and somehow life will take care of itself when you get back."

Baby Steps

It's a big step, stepping away from the security of the life you've always known and into the yawning abyss of a sabbatical. For some people, holding onto their job and taking just a short leave at first will be pretty easy to handle. But more importantly, it will whet the appetite for future, longer leaves, perhaps even without the safety net of a return job.

Understandably, at first, some of the men and women Neil Bull advises are reluctant to take the plunge. "I tell them they don't have to walk away for six months. Try two or three weeks first, because then you'll think about doing it again," he says.

Nella Barkley agrees and suggests that a person take a mini-sabbatical to help him decide how to spend the real thing. "Take a weekend and play some games with yourself, or with one or two close friends," she says. "If you were multiplying this weekend by a hundred days, what would it look like, and what would you want to come back with? Write down your answers," she advises, "because when you write, you start to anchor thoughts in a way that just doesn't happen when you're thinking about something."

Barkley even recommends that you take a pre-preliminary sabbatical approach: "Ask yourself why you'd want to take some time off from work. And then at least give yourself some regular time that is your own to think about your future in a positive way," she says.

Amy Hertz, who left her editorial job for five weeks, advises that people should take time off any way they can manage. She says that for many, it's a good idea to take a first leave without quitting a job. She adds that the best advice that anyone gave her when it came to deciding whether take a sabbatical was to tell her *not* to quit her job. "When you feel like quitting your job," she says, "it seems that's the time to take a leave of absence—before you do anything drastic."

But some people take drastic in stride and make it part of their lives. Either the sabbatical is only one of the more radical in a long line of risks that a person takes, or it's the first-ever high dive, which makes everything after that seem simple. However, even though you've made up your mind that you're definitely going to take the plunge, it doesn't necessarily mean your mind is going to be totally comfortable with the idea.

Five Ways to Get Up the Nerve
If You Have Cold Feet

1. Tell yourself you're going to die at the end of a year. How would you rather spend your time: working at your job or doing what you want to do?

2. Pretend that your sabbatical will be your new job for a while. Your first day of work is the target date that you've planned for your sabbatical. Then, all you have to do is report for your first day of "work."

3. Tell yourself in the beginning that if at the last minute you decide not to go through with your sabbatical, you will have to give the money you saved for it to your least favorite charity. For instance, if you're a dyed-in-the-wool liberal, then you'll have to donate the money to the most conservative right-wing organization you can find.

4. Do people think of you as staid, steady, predictable? It's always fun when people suddenly get a picture of you as an entirely different person. Let this drive you towards your goal.

5. Ask yourself if you'd really be happy doing what you're already doing for the rest of your life. Your sabbatical is the first step towards changing that.

Advice from the Pros

When it comes to looking for good advice, the best place you can turn to is the men and women who have already taken their sabbaticals and family leaves.

Start Planning Now

Debra Phillips, who spent ten years thinking about and planning her sabbatical, says that she's planning to take another sabbatical in 1997 or 1998 to write a book. She says that if she were to die tomorrow, she would appreciate the fact that she already was able to take one sabbatical. She uses this benchmark to give advice to people who ask her how they can take their own sabbaticals.

"When they ask me how I did it, I tell them to just plan for it, and figure out what they really want to do," she said. "If you were to die tomorrow, would you be sorry that you never took time off for yourself?"

Because she had to wait so long for her sabbatical, she suggests that people who want to take time off start planning it, even though the target date may be ten years away. Just starting to map out a plan for your time off will begin to make it more real to you. "A sabbatical gives you time off to evaluate where you are in your life, and where you want it to go," she said. "It was absolutely the most energizing experience of my life."

180 Degrees

Mariana Gosnell says that although some of her colleagues at the magazine took advantage of their leaves just to stay at home, she advises that people should really take advantage of this fantastic opportunity. "With that much time off, you should really make the most of it, and do something that you wouldn't ordinarily do on a vacation," she says. "Do something brand-new, and big or very different." One woman at the magazine spent three months just cleaning her apartment. "It makes me ill just to think of it," says Gosnell, although she adds that for some people, it's a good idea to do the kinds of things that they never have the time to do when they're working, like staying home with the kids and digging in their gardens.

Nick Leeming agrees with Gosnell's radical approach. "Find something totally different than the lifestyle you have now, preferably far away from home, where whatever you're doing is total immersion and you're doing it all alone," he says. "After all, that's the only way you're going to grow and learn a lot." He says that it's been his experience that the reason most people don't take some time off—whether it's before college or in the middle of a career—is that they don't know they can. "There's no reason why you have to start out in the world—or continue—at such a fast pace," he says.

Leeming says that he had his own litany of excuses that could easily have held him back from his sabbatical. "I was nervous about it, I didn't think that I'd want to go back to school after a year off, and I had no idea what I would gain from it," he recalls. "The important thing is that you shouldn't just take a year off and work at McDonald's or sit around and watch TV. Plan it out and stay busy the whole time. If you have to jump on a plane and work at an orphanage in Nepal, then do it."

Don't Wait Until You Retire

People frequently put off taking a breather from work because they figure that they'll have all the time in the world once they retire. They think that because they have the energy now, they should devote their working years to working.

Jordan Schaffel suggests that people who are thinking about taking time off during their working years think about those later retirement years, and consider whether they'll be healthy enough to enjoy them. "Look at how many years you have on the planet," he says. "Even if you could guarantee that you'll be healthy enough in later life to do what you want to do, you still wouldn't be able to travel steadily throughout the world like you could if you were younger."

What's Really Holding You Back?

In the end, if you're still hesitating, ask yourself this question: If all of your excuses not to take a sabbatical were taken away, then would you go? This question, more than any other, will get you to the real reason why you're not proceeding with your plans. Sometimes, the people who take time off and don't do anything constructive with it—although they did intend to achieve something significant during their sabbatical—have not dealt with their fears about leaving their jobs for a period of time. They believe, deep down, that they either don't deserve the time off or they can't fathom how the office will be able to survive without them. So they intentionally sabotage their time off so that they can say later that it wasn't worth it.

These are the people who need to develop a plan and then stick to it. Men and women who are used to being at a certain place at a certain time will sometimes wander around aimlessly if they haven't adequately planned their time off. The time will pass pretty quickly, and before they know it, it's time to go back to work, and they didn't accomplish what they set out to do.

Patience, too, is required. Neil Bull tells about a man he worked with who is stuck in a boring insurance job. Although he could rent out his house, he doesn't want to. Instead, he's going to wait until he can sell his house. He thinks that the only thing holding him back from taking a sabbatical is his mortgage, but he's not willing to take any other steps towards his sabbatical. "It costs him $45,000 a year to maintain a lifestyle in a house he doesn't want," says Neil. Shortly after his first meeting with Bull, he placed his house on the market. When the house sells, he'll meet up again with Bull and discuss how he wants to spend his time off. "People have to get to the point where they give themselves permission to do something of which society clearly disapproves. And sometimes that can take a long time," Bull says.

Giving Yourself Permission

Neil Bull says that the biggest challenge in his work is convincing people that they can take time off and survive to tell about it. "There's so much in our society that tells us not to make a move, and people themselves throw up many barriers at the same time," he says. "Because it's so alien to people, it takes some time to marinate about the things that you want to do, and then plan everything so that you have no choice but to make it happen."

You might eventually decide not to take off. But realizing that you have that option can make some of the interminable times at work easier.

However, as with everyone in this book, you shouldn't rule out the possibility of taking a sabbatical. "There's always a reason—or a hundred—not to take time off," says Noel Aderer. "But you have to ignore all that and totally change your orientation. Some people will have to admit that they just aren't up to it. But the first thing you have to do is make up your mind that you're going to do it, and everything else will follow.

Whether it involves foreign travel or staying put, your plans are made, the situation at the office is taken care of, and tomorrow's the big day: the first day of your sabbatical. You're incredibly excited about it and can't wait.

Yet, something is still holding you back. Even if you've

gotten this far in managing all of the logistical problems that can come from planning a sabbatical and have overcome all the obstacles put forth in this book, you're still a bit reluctant to go. What's swirling around in your head?

- ☐ This is selfish.
- ☐ This is so out of character for me.
- ☐ What if I don't like it?
- ☐ What if I like it too much?
- ☐ How will this change my life?
- ☐ What if I don't succeed?

Everyone whose sabbatical story appears in this book had the same last-minute conversations you're having now. And even though they may have postponed their sabbaticals for a few days or even longer, they did finally take the step from their regular lives to their sabbatical lives.

What it usually comes down to is telling yourself it's okay to do something so self-indulgent, or in the case of a social service leave, something so giving for a while.

Go ahead and give yourself permission. It may help if there are a few people around you who have already given you permission to go off on your adventure. And yes, this will probably turn out to be the biggest adventure of your life, simply because it is so different from anything else you've ever done.

I'm telling you that it's okay for you to go. If you have to say aloud to yourself "I give myself permission to take a sabbatical," even several hundred times before you begin to believe it, then do it. And who knows what will happen in your life because you took the chance. You may even end up like me, on sabbatical for the rest of your life.

Author's note: The author would like to hear about any sabbaticals that have resulted from the guidelines presented in this book for updates in future editions of *Time Off From Work*. Write with your experience to Lisa Angowski Rogak, c/o John Wiley & Sons, Inc., 605 Third Avenue, New York, NY 10158.

Appendix

Books

Axel, Helen. *Redefining Corporate Sabbaticals for the 1990s.* New York: The Conference Board, 1992.

Bolles, Richard N. *What Color is Your Parachute?: A Practical Manual for Job Hunters & Career Changers.* Berkeley, CA: Ten Speed Press, 1994.

Boyett, Joseph H., and Henry P. Conn, *Workplace Two Thousand: The Revolution Reshaping American Business.* New York: NAL-Dutton, 1991.

Germer, Jerry. *Country Careers: Successful Ways to Live and Work in the Country.* New York: John Wiley & Sons, Inc., 1993.

Glassner, Barry. *Career Crash: The End of America's Love Affair with Work.* New York: Simon & Schuster, 1994.

Goodwin, Daniel and Richard Rusdorf. *The Landlord's Handbook: A Complete Guide to Managing Small Residential Properties.* Chicago: Dearborn Financial Publishing, 1988.

Gosnell, Mariana. *Zero Three Bravo*. New York: Alfred A. Knopf, Inc., 1993.

Holloway, Diane and Nancy Bishop. *Before You Say, "I Quit": A Guide to Making Successful Job Transitions*. New York: Macmillan Publishing Company, 1990.

Kaye, Evelyn. *Travel & Learn: Where to Go for Everything You'd Love to Know*. 3rd ed. Boulder, CO: Blue Penguin Publications, 1994.

Levering, Robert and Milton Moskowitz. *The One Hundred Best Companies to Work For in America*. New York: NAL-Dutton, 1994.

McAdam, Terry W. *Doing Well by Doing Good: The First Complete Guide to Careers in the Nonprofit Sector*. New York: Penguin Books, 1988.

McDermott, Lynda C. *Caught in the Middle: How to Survive & Thrive in Today's Management Squeeze*. New York: Prentice-Hall, 1992.

New Ways to Work Staff and Julie Batz. *Work Sharing: An Alternative to Layoffs*. San Francisco: New Ways to Work, 1991.

Persoff, Albert Morton. *Sabbatical Years with Pay: A Plan to Create & Maintain Full Employment*. New York: Charter Publishing Company, 1945.

Pines, Ayala. *Career Burnout*. New York: Free Press, 1989.

Popcorn, Faith. *The Popcorn Report*. New York: Doubleday, 1991.

Scher, Les, and Carol Scher. *Finding & Buying Your Place in the Country*. Chicago: Dearborn Financial Publishing, 1992.

Sher, Barbara, and Barbara Smith. *I Could Do Anything If I Only Knew What It Was: How to Discover What You Really Want & How to Get It*. New York: Delacorte, 1994.

Skousen, Mark, and JoAnn Skousen. *High Finance on a Low Budget.* Chicago: Dearborn Financial Press, 1992.

Weisberg, Anne Cicero, and Carol A. Buckler. *Everything a Working Mother Needs to Know about Pregnancy Rights, Maternity Leave, & Making Her Career Work for Her.* New York: Doubleday, 1994.

Newsletters

Lonely Planet Newsletter
Lonely Planet Publications
155 Filbert Street
Oakland, CA 94607

The National Report on Work & Family
Buraff Publications/Millin Publications, Inc.
1350 Connecticut Avenue, NW
Washington, DC 20036

Sticks (for people who are serious about moving
    to the country)
Moose Mountain
RR1, Box 1234
Grafton, NH 03240

Work Times
New Ways to Work
149 Ninth Street
San Francisco, CA 94103

Working Options
The Association of Part-Time Professionals, Inc.
7700 Leesburg Pike, Suite 216
Falls Church, VA 22043

Associations

The Association of Part-Time Professionals, Inc.
7700 Leesburg Pike, Suite 216
Falls Church, VA 22043

The International Society for Work Options
c/o Focus
509 Tenth Avenue East
Seattle, WA 98118

National Association for the Self-Employed
P.O. Box 612067
DFW Airport, TX 75261-2067

New Ways to Work
149 Ninth Street
San Francisco, CA 94103

Workshare
311 East Fiftieth Street
New York, NY 10022

Major Corporations with Sabbatical and/or Social Service Leave Programs

Advanced Micro Devices
American Express Travel Related Services
Apple Computers
Du Pont Company
Genentech, Inc.
Hewitt Associates
Hewlett-Packard Company

IBM Corporation

Intel

Levi Strauss & Company

Lotus

McDonald's

Moog

Tandem Computers

Tennant

Time-Warner

U.S. Department of Justice

Wells Fargo & Company

Xerox

Counseling Centers

Center for Interim Programs
P.O. Box 2347
Cambridge, MA 02238
617-547-0980

Crystal-Barkley Corporation
Life/Work Design
152 Madison Avenue, 23rd Floor
New York, NY 10016
212-889-8500

Index